AWESOME FACTS

igloobooks

Published in 2015
by Igloo Books Ltd
Cottage Farm
Sywell
NN6 0BJ
www.igloobooks.com

SHE001 0715
2 4 6 8 10 9 7 5 3 1
ISBN 978-1-78440-787-2

Printed and manufactured in China

CONTENTS

The world is a wonderful place! Come on a journey of discovery, to find out about some of the amazing things that are going on all around you. Want to know about deep space and the beginning of the universe? Curious about Earth and natural disasters such as tornadoes and tsunamis? Ever wondered how your body works or how so many different kinds of animals and plants survive on our planet? The answers are all here. This book is also packed with awesome facts about science and technology and the latest inventions that are making the world even better. Once you start asking questions, you will not be able to stop!

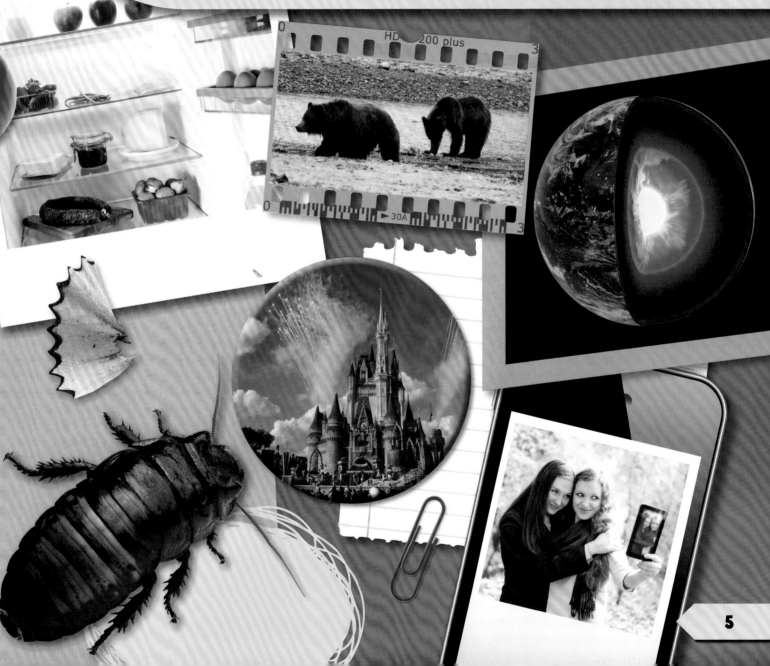

01

SPACE AND BEYOND

If you look up into the night sky, you will see a dazzling array of twinkling stars. That is space and it is vast. We can see only a tiny distance out into space with our eyes, but we know an amazing amount about what is happening out there in the dark. But how did it all begin? How did the stars and planets form? How do people explore space? Discover some of the secrets of the universe and find answers to all those burning questions.

OUR UNIVERSE

The universe is everything that exists, from Earth to the most distant parts of space. It is almost impossible to imagine how big and how awesome it is. The universe is mostly filled with empty space, but it also contains billions of galaxies, stars and other wonders. Experts working at the frontiers of science are trying to work out just what is out there.

Scientists think the universe began with an event called the Big Bang. This was a mega explosion that created all the matter and energy in the universe. The Big Bang took just a fraction of a second, but it was the beginning of time and space.

HOW OLD IS IT?

Scientists believe that the universe is about 13.7 billion years old. To calculate this, they measure the amount of microwave background radiation in space, which is left over from the Big Bang.

The **universe** has been **expanding** since the beginning of time. It is still expanding today. Everything is moving away from everything else. We know it is at least 93 billion light years across.

WHAT NEXT?

At first, the universe was incredibly hot. As it cooled over hundreds of thousands of years, particles joined together to form atoms, the building blocks of matter. After about one billion years, clouds of gas began to come together to form galaxies.

It is possible that the universe we observe is not everything that is out there. Some scientists think there is more than one universe and that there may be many bubbles of space-time that make up one great 'super universe'.

Outer space begins about 100 km (62 miles) above Earth, where the shell of air around our planet disappears. There is no air to scatter sunlight, so space looks like a black blanket dotted with millions of stars.

Space is not really empty. The areas between stars and planets are filled with huge amounts of gas and dust. Space also contains many forms of radiation, which are thrown out from distant star systems.

BLACK HOLES

Black holes are areas of space where matter has collapsed in on itself. The result is a huge amount of mass in an incredibly small area. The pull of gravity in this area is so strong that nothing can escape from it, not even light.

The universe is full of an unknown substance called 'dark matter'. Dark matter makes up about 85 per cent of all the matter in the universe.

SUCKED IN!

① We cannot see black holes, but we know they are there because of the way they affect nearby dust, stars and galaxies. Anything passing close to a black hole is sucked into it.

② In 2008, astronomers found a black hole with a mass 33 times bigger than the sun, in a dwarf galaxy called IC 10.

③ As matter spirals into a black hole, it is torn apart and glows so brightly that it creates the brightest objects in the universe, called quasars.

STARS IN YOUR EYES

Stars are born, grow old and die, just like people. Unlike for us, however, the life cycle of a star takes many billions of years! Along the way, stars make some incredible displays in space. Astronomers are using cutting-edge science to discover more about these marvels.

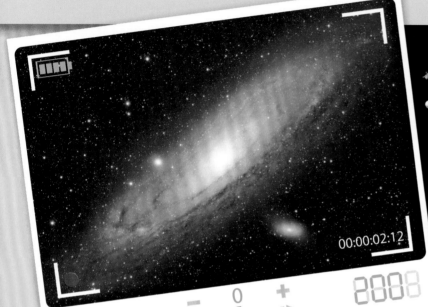

00:00:02:12

About 100 million years after the Big Bang, the clouds of dust and gas became hot and dense enough for stars to form. Clusters of stars slowly joined to make **galaxies**.

The Hubble Space Telescope has found galaxies that were formed about 100 million years after the Big Bang. They were closer together than most galaxies are today.

BILLIONS OF BILLIONS

There are billions of galaxies in the universe. About three-quarters of them are spirals, with curved arms wrapped round a bright, central core. Each galaxy contains billions of stars.

New stars are surrounded by a huge flat disc of gas and dust. When some of this material combines, planets are formed. Planets begin to orbit around the star.

DENSEST GALAXIES

The densest galaxies are called Ultra Compact Dwarf Galaxies. They were discovered in 1999. They contain about a billion stars in a space that is 200 light years across. Astronomers think that billions of years ago, they were even denser than that.

RED GIANTS

Stars take millions of years to die. Once a star has burned all its fuel, it expands and becomes a red giant.

The **red supergiant Antares** is 800 times wider than the sun. If it were in the middle of our solar system, it would swallow up all the inner planets, including Earth.

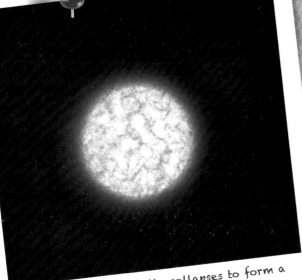

A red giant eventually collapses to form a **white dwarf**. One teaspoon of material from a white dwarf would weigh up to 100 tonnes (110 tons), the same as about 50 rhinos!

MILKY WAY

Our galaxy, the Milky Way, formed when smaller galaxies came together to make a bigger one.

Material blasts away from the site of a **supernova** at about 50 million kph (31 million mph). That is fast enough to travel from Earth to the moon in 30 seconds!

SUPERNOVA

Some red giants swell into supergiants. After a few million years, they blow up in an explosion called a supernova. One of the last supernovae in our galaxy took place about 340 years ago. It was 10,000 light years from Earth.

Did you know?

Supernovae spread stardust across galaxies. Almost everything on Earth is made from elements that came from this stardust, including people!

11

OUR SOLAR SYSTEM

Our solar system lies in one of the arms of a large spiral galaxy called the Milky Way. It is about halfway out from the middle of the galaxy. It consists of a star (the sun) and eight planets. The planets are Mercury, Venus, Earth, Mars, Jupiter, Saturn, Uranus and Neptune. They orbit the Sun.

The Milky Way rotates once every 200 million years. It contains at least 100 billion stars and its light takes 100,000 years to cross from one side to the other.

KUIPER BELT

Beyond the orbit of Neptune is the Kuiper belt. This is a band of objects left over from the formation of the planets.

Until recently, the furthest-known planet was **Pluto**, an icy world at the edge of the solar system. Scientists now think it is too small to be called a true planet. It is even smaller than our moon. Pluto is now called a dwarf planet, and more of them have been found.

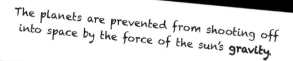
The planets are prevented from shooting off into space by the force of the sun's gravity.

ASTEROID BELT

Between Mars and Jupiter lies an asteroid belt, which is full of millions of rocky objects.

In 2005, an icy object at least as big as Pluto was discovered in our solar system, very far from the sun. Astronomers have named it **Eris**.

12

The twinkling of stars in the sky is caused by Earth's **atmosphere**. The atmosphere bends and breaks up the faint light from the stars before it reaches our eyes.

OUT AT THE EDGE

The Oort Cloud of comets lies even further away than the Kuiper belt. These comets become visible to us in the night sky only if they are disturbed and head towards the sun.

00:00:02:12

The largest moon in the solar system is Jupiter's moon, Ganymede.

NEW PLANETS

① Astronomers are looking for planets orbiting other stars in other solar systems in the Milky Way. So far, they have found more than 1,900. They are called extrasolar planets.

② The distance to the planets is measured by bouncing radar signals off them and timing how long the signals take to travel there and back.

Ceres is the **biggest asteroid** in the solar system. It is 940 km (584 miles) across. That's nearly 9,000 football pitches! The Dawn space probe reached Ceres in March 2015 after a journey of more than 7 years!

OUR SUN

The sun is a huge ball of super-hot gas. It is a star, but we never see it at night. It produces the light and heat that make life on our planet possible. Without it, our world would be frozen and dark. When our part of Earth is facing the sun we have day, and when it faces away, we have night.

The sun is 1.4 million km (0.8 million miles) across. That is about 109 planet Earths side by side!

There are some areas on the sun's surface that are slightly cooler than others. These areas are called **sun spots**.

Sometimes, the sun's energy moves up through the outer layers and shoots out in huge jets of flames called **flares**.

THAT IS MASSIVE!

The sun weighs about 300,000 times as much as Earth, even though it is made almost entirely of hydrogen and helium, the lightest gases in the universe.

The hottest part of the sun is its **core**. As the gases move out from the core, they get a bit cooler and heavier, but not much.

Solar flares reach temperatures of 10 million °C (50 million F) and have the energy of 1 million atom bombs.

ECLIPSE

If the moon gets directly between Earth and the sun, it blocks the sun's light on Earth for a few moments. It goes dark in the daytime. This is called an eclipse.

00:00:02:12

Solar flares can interact with Earth's magnetic field to create light shows known as the Northern and Southern lights.

SUNSET AND SUN RISE

The sun is so far away that its light takes about 8 minutes to reach Earth. When we see a sunset, it actually happened about 8 minutes ago.

SPACECRAFT APPROACHING

In 1976, Helios 2 came within 43.5 million km (27 million miles) of the sun. This is the closest approach to the sun by any spacecraft.

In December 1995, the **SOHO** (Solar and Heliospheric Observatory) probe was launched from Cape Canaveral, Florida, to study the sun.

It is about 150 million km (93 million miles) to the sun from planet Earth!

15

EARTH AND MOON

The closest object to Earth is its moon. The moon is much nearer to Earth than any of the planets. It travels around Earth and makes one complete orbit of our planet every 27.3 days.

Earth takes 365 days (a year) to rotate once around the sun. It travels at a **speed** of 108,000 kph (67,000 mph).

ATMOSPHERE

Earth is the only planet with an atmosphere that contains oxygen and liquid water and can support life.

Earth is the only planet in the solar system that is not **named after** a Roman or Greek god.

It takes Earth 24 hours (a day) to **rotate** once on its axis.

A PERFECT SPHERE?

People used to think the Earth was flat, but then they learned that it is round. Actually, it is not perfectly round either. It bulges slightly in the middle and is flatter at the top and bottom.

The moon is held in place in its orbit by the **force** of **gravity** on Earth. The moon has its own gravity, too, though it is less than that on Earth.

The moon is about 50 times smaller than Earth. It is covered with rocks and dust.

00:00:02:12

From Earth, the **moon** seems to shine but it does not produce light of its own. Instead, it reflects light from the sun.

There is no air or water on the moon. Without air, there is no weather. The footprints left by astronauts almost 50 years ago, are still untouched.

WATER WATER

Nearly two-thirds of Earth is covered with water. Of that, 97 per cent is salty and only 3 per cent is fresh water, most of which is frozen.

The average surface **temperature** of the moon during the day is 107 °C (225 F). The moon is so hot because it has no atmosphere to protect it from the sun's heat.

ROCKY PLANETS

Mercury, Venus and Mars are the planets nearest Earth. They are all rocky planets and they can all be seen with the naked eye from Earth. We have been very successful at sending space probes to find out what they are like.

MARS A DAY

It takes Mars 687 Earth days to orbit the sun and this planet has seasons like ours. Scientists think that primitive life forms might once have existed on Mars, but there are no Martians there now.

RED SOIL

The red appearance of Mars is due to rusted iron in its soil.

The highest mountain in the solar system is the Martian volcano **Olympus Mons**. It is 25 km (16 miles) high. That is nearly three times the height of Earth's Mount Everest.

Did you know?

There is a plan for a manned mission to Mars in the future, but if you want to apply, you have to be prepared for a one-way ticket. It takes so long to get there that there are no plans to return to Earth!

00:00:02:12

8888

A day on **Mercury** lasts about as long as 59 days on Earth.

ARTY CRATERS

The surface of Mercury is covered with craters caused by the impact of asteroids and comets. Many of these craters have been named after artists and writers.

The clouds hiding the solid surface of **Venus** are full of poisonous gases and acid. Under them, it is hot enough to melt many metals. It is definitely not a place for astronauts to land.

In 2008, the **Messenger** spacecraft passed by Mercury within just 200 km (124 miles) of its surface.

GOING BACKWARDS?

Most planets rotate anti-clockwise on their axes, but Venus and Uranus rotate clockwise.

MAPPING VENUS

The *Magellan* space probe was sent to Venus in 1989 to map its surface. It showed that it is mostly covered in volcanic lava. After its mission, it was allowed to break up in space.

THE GIANTS

Jupiter and Saturn are the two giants of the solar system. Both are about ten times bigger than Earth around their middles. You could never land on these planets because they are not solid. They are huge balls of gas and liquid, with a core of solid rock.

Jupiter has 67 known moons. Jupiter's moon Ganymede is bigger than the planet Mercury.

The biggest storm on Jupiter is called the **Great Red Spot**. The Great Red Spot is a vast whirlwind bigger than Earth.

Jupiter's moon Io is covered with erupting volcanoes, while another of its moons, called **Europa**, is covered in ice.

Jupiter is the **biggest planet**. It is also the heaviest, with a mass two-and-a-half times the mass of all the other planets combined!

FOREVER CLOUDY

Jupiter is covered with layers of clouds that look like bands around it. They are constantly blown about by gales and hurricanes.

FIRST SIGHT

Galileo Galilei was the first person to see four of Jupiter's moons with a telescope, back in 1610.

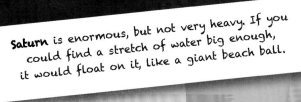

Saturn is enormous, but not very heavy. If you could find a stretch of water big enough, it would float on it, like a giant beach ball.

RINGS AND THINGS

Saturn is easy to spot because of its **rings**. There are at least seven rings spinning around its middle. The rings are made up of millions of pieces of rock and ice. They stretch out for about 241,000 km (150,000 miles).

AWESOME SATURN

① Saturn has more than 30 moons. The biggest so far discovered is called Titan.

Saturn is 1,427 million km (887 million miles) from the sun and takes more than 29 Earth years to orbit the sun once.

② Saturn was visited by the *Cassini* orbiter in 2005. It took 7 years to get there. *Cassini* also landed on Titan in 2005 and sent back a lot of information about it.

OUT ON THE EDGE

Uranus and Neptune are the planets furthest from the sun. They are known as the ice giants. You need a powerful telescope to see them because they are an unbelievably long way away. It is incredibly cold out there.

Uranus lies more than 2,800 million km (1,740 million miles) from the sun. It is 19 times further from the sun than Earth is.

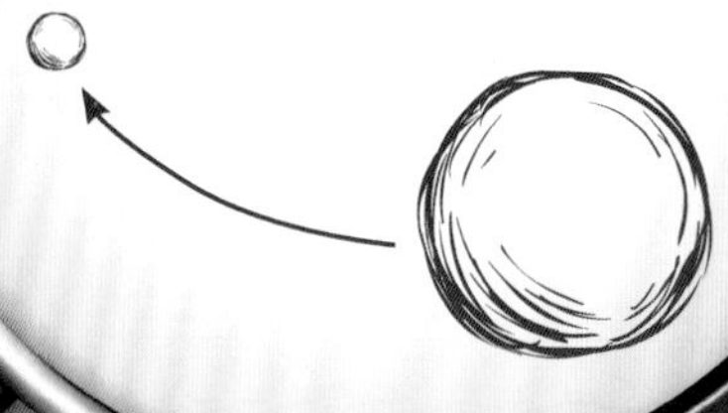

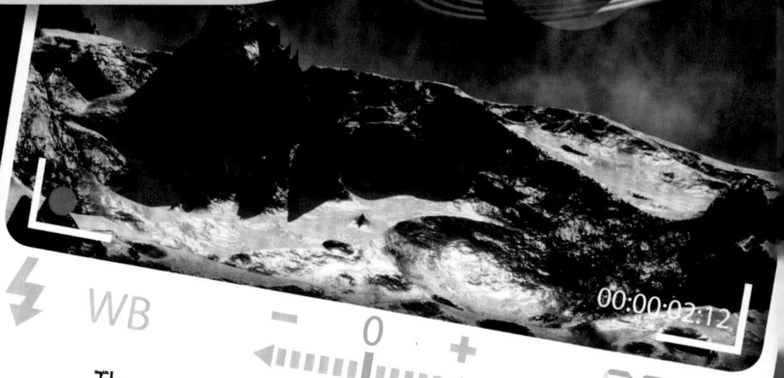

WB — 0 +

ISO

The average **temperature** on Uranus is −212°C (−350 F). It is the coldest planet in the solar system.

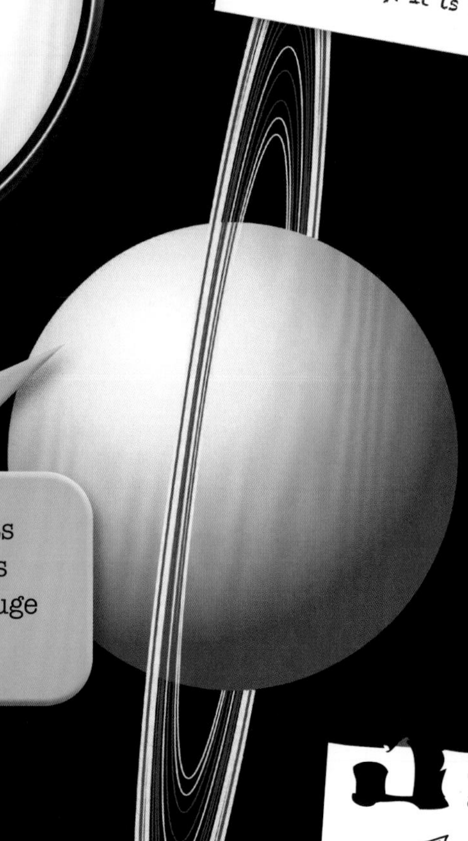

Uranus spins like a top on its side, probably because it was knocked sideways when a huge lump of rock crashed into it.

It takes **Uranus** 30,685 Earth days to orbit the sun once. Some parts of it are dark for more than 40 years at a time.

PREDICTING PLANETS

Neptune was the first planet whose existence was mathematically predicted before it was seen through a telescope. Later, in 1846, Johann Galle saw the planet for the first time through a telescope. The planet was named after the Roman god of the sea.

NEPTUNE'S MOONS

Neptune has 14 moons. The biggest is Triton. It is so cold there that even the volcanoes are frozen.

Neptune is the stormiest planet. The wind there can reach speeds of 1,996 kph (1,240 mph). That is more than three times the speed of hurricanes on Earth.

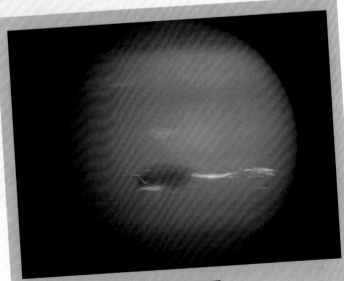

THE BLUE PLANET

Neptune is bright blue. It is made up of gas, ice and water and has a rocky core.

GETTING THERE

The first spacecraft to reach the outer planets was Voyager 2. It launched in 1977 and took 9 years to reach Uranus.

A LEAP INTO SPACE

People have always been fascinated with the night sky and have wondered what was out there. It is only in the last 50 years or so that they have been able to travel into space to have a look for themselves. In that time, we have learned a huge amount.

The first man in space was a Russian cosmonaut named **Yuri Gagarin**. In 1961 he blasted off in a rocket.

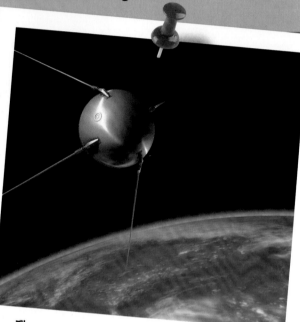

The **space age** began in 1957 when Russia launched the *Sputnik* satellite. Later that year, a satellite carried a dog, Laika, into space.

LIVING IN SPACE

The International Space Station (ISS) is the biggest object ever flown in space. It has been under construction since its first component was launched in November 1998. Astronauts travel there to live and work for a few months at a time.

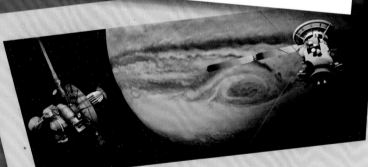

VISITING THE PLANETS

Since 1962, probes have been sent to all the planets. Some have landed on the planets, on Mars, for example. Others have flown past to collect data and take photographs.

A series of unmanned spacecraft take supplies to and from the **ISS**, such as fuel, food and equipment.

NO SPEED LIMIT!

The ISS travels at more than 27,000 kph (16,700 mph). It is 400 km (250 miles) above our heads. That's as high as the river Thames is long! You can see it in the night sky. It looks like a moving star.

The most remote human-made object in space is a spacecraft launched in the 1970s, *Voyager 1*. It has been in space for more than 38 years and has covered an enormous distance.

The spacecraft **Voyager 1** communicates through radio waves, but no one is sure exactly where it is right now. Some think it has already left the solar system and reached interstellar space! It should keep going until the 2020s.

The project **SETI** (Search for Extraterrestrial Intelligence) studies radio signals from space for signs of intelligent life.

The full cost of a **spacesuit** is about US $11 million (about £7 million), although most of this is for the backpack and the control module.

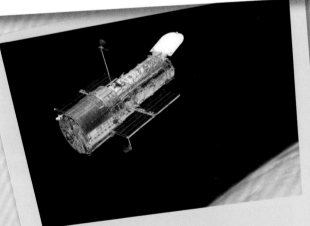

OBSERVATORIES

We learn about space from space observatories such as the Hubble Space Telescope. They look into the universe and send back pictures.

HOW FAR CAN WE GO?

All the time, scientists are working on ways to probe deeper into space and find out more. They are looking for planets around other stars, where there may even be other forms of life. The twenty-first century will be an exciting time in space exploration!

Up to now, chemical fuels have powered almost all space missions. To travel a long way takes a lot of heavy fuel. A new kind of engine, an **ion engine**, uses an electric 'gun' to fire gas into space. It gradually builds to a high speed.

Another way to travel far into space is to use huge '**solar sails**' on spacecraft. These would use energy from the sun to push the craft forward at a great speed.

GOING NUCLEAR

For missions far from the sun, scientists think that nuclear engines will be needed. With one of these, it might be possible to reach Mars in just a few days.

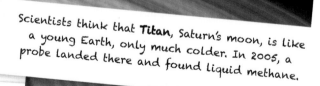

Scientists think that **Titan**, Saturn's moon, is like a young Earth, only much colder. In 2005, a probe landed there and found liquid methane.

EXTRASOLAR PLANETS

Planets in other solar systems are called extrasolar planets. Several hundred have been found so far. We are beginning to work out what their atmospheres are made of, and if they could support life.

A new space telescope to replace Hubble, the **James Webb Space Telescope**, will be launched in 2018.

HUBBLE TROUBLE

The Hubble Space Telescope is the only one that is serviced in space by astronauts. It has been repaired many times but cannot last forever. Plans to bring it back to Earth have changed. It will now stay out in space even after it has stopped working, in about 2020.

SATELLITES

Thousands of satellites are sent into space. We use them for communications, weather forecasting and many other things. Our world would not work without them.

In 2006, Europe's **Corot** spacecraft was launched. It is looking for changes that are happening to stars and new worlds. So far, it has studied 120,000 stars!

Did you know?

The 'nearest' star to Earth (after the sun) is Alpha Centauri, but it is about 4 light years away, or 40 trillion km (24 trillion miles).

PLANET EARTH

Our world is a beautiful place. It looks round and calm from space, but down here there are mountains, oceans, rivers and canyons. Sometimes, the world is battered by extreme weather and catastrophic natural disasters. It is a changing world, too. Humans are affecting every part of it and people need to understand how the planet works so that it can be preserved for the future.

02

LAND AND SEA

The Earth is covered in land, sea and ice. After the planet formed, the land began to settle into huge shapes called tectonic plates. These plates moved around, split up and joined together again many times. This created our landscape of land and sea, mountains, valleys and rivers. The plates are still moving, but they do this incredibly slowly.

Scientists have dated Earth as being between 4 and 5 billion years old.

FLOATING

The Earth is covered in islands surrounded by sea. The largest island is Greenland, which is in the Arctic Circle.

Hawaii, an island in the Pacific, is moving towards Japan at a speed of 10 cm (4 in) a year. This is because their landmasses are on different tectonic plates.

ROLLING RIVER

Stretching out to an impressive length of 6,696 km (4,160 miles), the Nile, in Africa, is the longest river on Earth.

LOVELY LAKES

The deepest lake in the world is Lake Baikal in Russia. It is 1,741 m (5,712 ft) deep, which is more than twice the height of the world's tallest building.

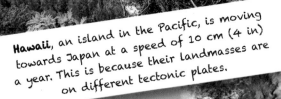

Mount Everest, in the Himalayan Mountains in Nepal, is the highest mountain on Earth. Its peak reaches 8,848 m (29,029 ft) above sea level.

The **Andes** is the world's longest mountain range. It is about 7,600 km (4,700 miles) long and spans seven South American countries.

The highest waterfall in the world is the incredible **Angel Falls** in Venezuela.

DOWN BELOW

Moving landmasses create caves as well as mountains. The deepest cave is the Krubera Cave in Georgia. Its deepest explored point is 2,191 m (7,188 ft) underground.

CONTINENTAL

About 1 billion years ago, there was just one super-continent, called Rodinia. Today, it is broken into seven continents: Asia, Africa, North America, South America, Europe, Antarctica and Oceania. Asia is the largest continent.

The five **oceans** of the world are the Pacific, Atlantic, Indian, Southern and Arctic. The Pacific is the biggest by far.

EARTH'S OUTER LAYER

The outside of Earth is made of different kinds of rock. These rocks contain all sorts of minerals and other materials that we use for building and for making things. All these amazing resources make modern life possible and humans are constantly looking for new ways to use them.

Earth is solid on the outside, but it is not solid all the way through. The **outer crust** varies from 5 km to 70 km (3 miles to 44 miles) thick. It is thinner under the sea and thicker on land.

Many amazing buildings have been created using stone. The **Taj Mahal** in India is made of marble, which is a very hard stone.

SOFT ROCK

Below the Earth's crust is the mantle, made of red-hot rocks. Some of them are melted and the layer below that is even more liquid. At the core is a solid, incredibly dense ball.

The ground is full of **metals**, such as iron, copper and tin. Metals are strong and very useful for construction. They are also good conductors of heat and electricity. Some are precious and used to make decorative things like necklaces and brooches. These precious jewels are called **minerals**.

The biggest nugget of gold ever discovered is the **Holtermann Nugget**, found in a mine in Australia in 1872. It weighed 235 kg (518 lb), which is as much as two sheep!

GOLDEN TENNIS

Gold can be beaten into very thin sheets. If you filled a matchbox with gold, it could be flattened into a sheet the size of a tennis court.

HARD OR SOFT?

Minerals vary a lot in how hard they are. The softest mineral is talc and the hardest is wurtzite boron nitride. Silicon is a mineral used to make the mircochips in computers.

THAT'S A ROCK!

The biggest diamond ever discovered was the Cullinan diamond. It was found in a mine in South Africa in 1905.

Most metals are solid at room temperature, but **mercury** is liquid.

METAL

The metal that is found the most often in the Earth's crust is aluminium.

MOVING EARTH

You are standing outside and suddenly the ground beneath your feet starts to move... It shakes more violently and everything around you is moving, too. It is an earthquake! There are small earthquakes, or tremors, happening somewhere in the world all the time, but when a big one hits, it can be a major disaster.

MEASURING QUAKES

① Scientists measure earthquakes using the Richter scale. It measures the amount of energy released during an earthquake. A hand grenade releases energy equivalent to 0.2 on the Richter scale. The earthquake responsible for the Indian Ocean tsunami of 2004 measured 9.2 on the Richter scale.

② The power and effects of earthquakes are measured by seismologists. The power of the vibrations is measured and shown on a chart called a seismometer.

DISASTER!

In a major earthquake, the movement of the Earth makes buildings, bridges and other structures collapse. Everyone is in danger.

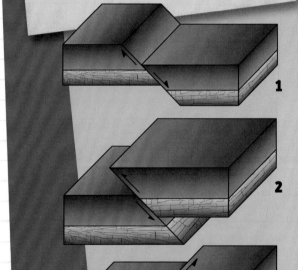

1

2

3

Tectonic plates move in three main ways. Sometimes, two plates gradually move apart (1). Sometimes they move towards each other and one plate gradually slides under the other (2). Two tectonic plates can also grind past each other in opposite directions (3). All three kinds of movement cause violent earthquakes.

RING OF FIRE

Some of the world's worst earthquakes occur in the Pacific Ocean along a line of weakness in the Earth's crust called the Ring of Fire. This zone encircles the Pacific Ocean, from Alaska, North America, down the west coasts of North and South America, and up along the east coasts of Asia. Japan lies on the Ring of Fire.

In March 2011, an earthquake struck off the northeastern coast of **Japan**. It measured 9.0 on the Richter scale. Bridges, roads and buildings across the country were destroyed.

SAN FRANCISCO QUAKE

During the massive earthquake in San Francisco, California in 1906, more than 80 per cent of the city was destroyed. People then learned how to design cities and buildings to better withstand the shocks of earthquakes.

On 26th December 2004, a massive earthquake struck off the northwestern coast of **Sumatra**. It was the third-most powerful earthquake in recorded history. Measuring about 9.2 on the Richter scale, it released the same amount of energy as 23,000 atomic bombs going off at the same time. The shock waves of the quake were felt as far afield as South Africa and Mexico.

CHANGING NATURE

In 1811 and 1812, three earthquakes measuring around 8.0 on the Richter scale caused the Mississippi River in the United States to flow backwards. These earthquakes also created Reelfoot Lake in Tennessee.

ERUPTIONS!

Volcanoes are one of Earth's most impressive and deadly displays. Deep under Earth's surface are pockets of hot, melted rock. If there is a crack in the surface, this very hot rock forces its way up and out of the crack.

In an eruption, melted rock, called **lava**, comes spewing out of the crack and flows away. It gradually cools and hardens into new rock. This piles up around the crack to form a volcano. A volcano will erupt many times over the centuries, growing bigger after each eruption.

KRAKATOA

In 1883, the Indonesian island of Krakatoa was destroyed by a series of four massive volcanic eruptions that blew it apart. The collapse of the island created a series of massive tsunamis that struck land as far away as South Africa. More than 36,000 people lost their lives and the huge cloud of ash it created blotted out the sun for two whole days.

It is not just lava that pours out of an erupting volcano. Massive clouds of **ash**, **dust** and poisonous **gas** are created, too.

The eruption of Krakatoa in 1883 made one of the loudest noises ever. People heard it 5,000 km (3,100 miles) away!

Lava flows quite slowly so it rarely kills people. Most people killed by erupting volcanoes are suffocated by the hot gas and ash that sweep across the land at speeds of up to 200 kph (125 mph). They may also be hit by flying 'bombs' of rock.

In CE 79 in southern Italy, a volcano called **Mount Vesuvius** erupted, killing everyone in the city of Pompeii in a very short time. They were killed by the poisonous gas. Pompeii remained buried beneath ash for hundreds of years.

NO-FLY ZONE

Mauna Loa in Hawaii is the largest active volcano on Earth. From the base to the top, it is more than 17,000 m (56,000 ft).

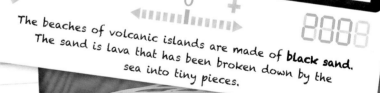

The beaches of volcanic islands are made of **black sand**. The sand is lava that has been broken down by the sea into tiny pieces.

VOLCANO-FREE ZONE

There are no active volcanoes in Australia. This is mainly because there are no tectonic plate boundaries in Australia.

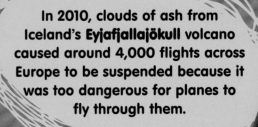

In 2010, clouds of ash from Iceland's **Eyjafjallajökull** volcano caused around 4,000 flights across Europe to be suspended because it was too dangerous for planes to fly through them.

SCARY TSUNAMIS

A tsunami is a major disaster! Tsunamis are caused when earthquakes happen under the sea. The shock of the earthquake shakes up the water and makes huge waves. They race to the shore, where they cause terrible damage to people and property.

A tsunami has more than one wave; the **waves** just keep on coming. They spread out from the earthquake like ripples on a pond but they are much more deadly.

In March 2011, **Japan** was hit by a tsunami. The tallest waves to reach the shore were 38 m (125 ft), about the same height as a building 10 floors high.

FAST FORCE

Tsunami waves travel across the ocean at speeds of up to 960 kph (600 mph). That is as fast as a passenger jet.

ACROSS THE LAND

Tsunami waves surge inland and take everything in their path with them. In Japan in 2011, they reached up to 10 km (6 miles) inland. Whole villages and towns were flattened.

WALLS OF WATER

In deep water, tsunami waves are not very big, but as they approach the shore, they slow down and grow into walls of water.

On 26th December 2004, an **earthquake** under the Indian Ocean caused a tsunami. Indonesia, India, Sri Lanka and Thailand were affected and more than 285,000 people were killed.

The 2011 tsunami that hit Japan produced 2 m (7 ft) **wave surges** as far away as California and Oregon in the United States.

Tsunamis have a terrible **power**. They cause total destruction on coasts and islands. The places affected by one tsunami may be very far apart, as the waves spread out across the ocean from their source.

ROCKS FROM SPACE

Meteorites are pieces of rock flying in space. If one crashed into an ocean, it would create a giant tsunami. Scientists think this happened 3.5 billion years ago. The waves swept around the world and destroyed much of the life on our planet.

Tsunamis used to be called **tidal waves**, but they are not connected with the tides of the ocean at all. Tides are partly a result of the gravitational pull of the moon.

'Tsunami' is a Japanese word that translates into English as 'harbour wave'.

WORLDWIDE WEATHER

Our weather happens in the atmosphere, the band of air around the Earth. Weather can be very different depending on where in the world you live. Most parts of the world have several seasons through the year. In other places, the weather is the same most of the time. Wherever you live, sometimes it is just extreme!

RAIN, RAIN GO AWAY

The place where it rains more than anywhere else on Earth is Mawsynram, in India. In a typical year, Mawsynram gets 1,187 cm (467.4 in) of rain.

The wind can make air feel colder than it is. This is called the **wind chill factor**. In -23 °C (-9.4 F), if the wind is blowing at 40 kph (24 mph) it will feel more like -51 °C (-60 F).

Hail is frozen raindrops that form in thunderclouds. In 1986, Bangladesh was hit by some of the biggest hailstones ever recorded. They weighed 1 kg (2.2 pounds) each.

Snowflakes form when water droplets freeze into ice crystals. Snowflakes are always six-sided, but there are 1 trillion, trillion, trillion (a 1 with 36 zeros) different shapes that they can be, so you are not likely to find two exactly the same!

One of the driest places in the world is **Calama** in Chile. Until 1971, there had been no rain there for 400 years.

DEATH VALLEY

Temperatures are usually measured in the air, but if they are measured on the ground they can be much hotter. A ground temperature of 93.9 °C (201 F) was recorded in Death Valley, California, on 15th July 1972 – that's hot enough to fry an egg! The world's hottest air temperature was measured there, too. In July 1913, it reached 56.7 °C (134 F)!

The coldest places on Earth are at the **North and South Poles**. In Antarctica, the temperature has been as low as −89.2 °C (−128.6 F). That is the record for the coldest place ever.

ALIENS FROM SPACE?

People have often thought that strange weather events were signs of magic or the supernatural. One kind of cloud, called a lenticular cloud, looks just like an alien flying saucer!

SEEING WHAT IS COMING

① Today, scientists can predict the weather using satellites in space. These hover 36,000 km (22,370 miles) up, to take photos and measure temperatures on Earth's surface.

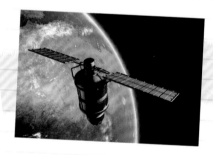

② On the ground, radar is used to detect patterns in the clouds and work out which way they are heading. Radar waves are sent out to bounce off the raindrops in the clouds and come back to giant radar dishes on the ground.

SUPER STORMS

A dramatic thunderstorm is really exciting, as long as you are not out in it. Storms are some of nature's most amazing ways of showing us its power. Darkening skies, strong winds and torrential rain or snow all remind us that the weather can be incredibly wild.

Tall black clouds full of rain contain a powerful charge of electricity. When the clouds move closer together, or near the ground, giant sparks of electricity fly between them. We see them as flashes of **lightning**. Thunder is the noise made by the hot air expanding around the sparks of lightning.

Tall buildings and monuments are frequently hit by **lightning**. If you are out in a storm, make sure you are not the tallest object around and never stand under trees.

Light travels faster than sound, so we see **flashes of lightning** before we hear the rumble of the thunder.

BLIZZARD!

If a storm happens when it is snowing heavily, this is called a blizzard. The strong winds blow the snow into deep drifts.

AROUND THE WORLD

About 45,000 thunderstorms happen around the world every day, so one is happening somewhere every minute.

Wind storms such as **tornadoes** and **hurricanes** happen when the wind spirals out of control. These are the fastest winds on Earth and they can cause complete destruction.

There have been reports of it '**raining frogs**'. This happens when tornadoes suck up frogs or other animals and then move away, dropping the animals somewhere else.

AGAIN AND AGAIN

The worst ever tornado outbreak was in April 2011. In just 24 hours, 207 tornadoes hit six states of the United States.

Hurricanes are huge wind storms. They form in warm and wet conditions, usually over the sea in tropical parts of the world. When they hit land, they cause massive damage.

A **whiteout** is an extreme kind of blizzard, or snowstorm. Whiteouts happen in storms with dry, powdery snow that flies about in strong winds. During a whiteout, it is impossible to see and very dangerous to be outside.

In 2005, **Hurricane Katrina** hit the city of New Orleans on the east coast of the USA. At least 1,800 people died and the damage cost more than US $100 billion to repair.

43

NORTH AND SOUTH: THE POLES

At the top and bottom of the world are the polar regions. The area around the North Pole is called the Arctic, while the area around the South Pole is called the Antarctic. It is below freezing there most of the time, and covered in ice, but there is still a lot happening.

HOT OR COLD

A desert is a place where it hardly ever rains or snows. It does not have to be hot. The Antarctic is the coldest desert in the world.

COLD SEASONS

The Poles both have two seasons: a long, cold winter and a short, slightly less cold summer!

The **Antarctic** is a continent entirely surrounded by oceans, but the **Arctic** is an ocean almost entirely surrounded by continents.

PENGUINS IN THE SUN

Antarctica is freezing today, but millions of years ago it had a very hot climate. The Antarctic landmass was on the equator.

There is no pole in the ground at the **North Pole**! It is the very top point of the sphere that is Earth.

The Earth is magnetic, as if it had a huge magnetic bar through the middle. The ends of the 'magnet' are called the **magnetic poles**. They are not in exactly the same position as the North Pole and South Pole, but they are not too far away.

TUNDRA

In summer in the Arctic, enough of the ice melts for the land to become visible. It is called the tundra and it is covered with low-growing plants and flowers.

Polar bears are found in the Arctic. They are the largest meat-eating animals on Earth.

OVER THE POLE

The first ever flight over the North Pole took place in May 1926 in an airship with a Norwegian pilot and 15 crew.

BURIED TREASURE

Buried under 4 km (2.5 miles) of ice in the eastern Antarctic is one of the oldest and cleanest lakes on Earth, Lake Vostok. The lake has been isolated from the rest of the world for at least 500,000 years.

WHERE ON EARTH?

The regions of the world provide many different kinds of habitat. There are forests and jungles, grasslands and deserts. The weather is different in each one, and the landscape, too, but there are stunning geographical features to see wherever you go.

Grasslands cover more than one-fifth of the Earth's land surface. They have different names in different parts of the world. In East Africa, they are hot savannahs. In Southern Africa, they are called veld. In North America, they are the prairies, and in Central Europe and Asia, they are known as steppes.

TREES FOREVER

Plants are incredibly important for keeping Earth healthy, especially big ones like trees. All plants release oxygen into the air, and take harmful carbon dioxide out of it. We need the oxygen that rainforests and woodlands put into the atmosphere.

RAINFORESTS

Rainforests grow in tropical places. The weather there is the same all year round (hot and wet). The trees and plants grow thick and close together and some of them reach incredible heights.

Over the last century, a lot of the prairies of North America and steppes of Central Europe have been ploughed and turned into farmland for growing food.

The **rainforest floor** gets very little light because the tall trees block it out.

Deserts are tough places to live. There is little rain there. In hot deserts, the sun beats down constantly from a cloudless sky.

When we think of the desert we think of **sand dunes**, but only about one-fifth of the world's deserts are covered in sand. Mostly, they are covered in gravel and rocks.

00:00:02:12

In some desert places, the **wind-blown sand** has worn away the rocks and mountains to form strange shapes.

The overall length of the world's **coastline** is 350,016 km (217,490 miles), roughly the same distance as from Earth to the moon, or almost nine times round Earth!

COASTS

With so much of Earth being seas, the planet has a lot of coasts! These are places where the land meets the sea. They may have cliffs or wide sandy beaches, endless sunshine or wild and windy storms.

AMAZING WORLD

We are putting enormous pressure on the world's resources. Everyone needs a safe place to live and to have access to water and food, work and money. Earth has limited resources and the modern world is stretching them to breaking point. We need to take better care of our planet so that it can continue to support us.

Greenhouse gases trap heat in the Earth's atmosphere and warm the planet. If they continue to build up, they will warm the Earth too much.

TAKE THE BUS!

There are more than 1 billion cars on the roads around the world! They are all polluting the atmosphere and contributing to climate change. Next time you travel, why not take a bicycle, a bus or a train instead.

TOO MUCH CARBON DIOXIDE

① Today, the amount of carbon dioxide in the atmosphere is higher than at any time in the last 650,000 years. This is causing the Earth's temperature to rise.

② We release carbon dioxide into the atmosphere by burning coal and gas, from our car engines and from polluting factories.

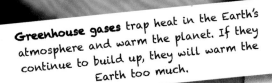

Even a small rise in **temperature** has huge effects. The ice at the Poles melts, raising sea levels and causing flooding. The world's weather patterns change, too, making some places much hotter.

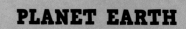

In the rich parts of the world, people have more than enough to eat, but in other parts, millions of people are **hungry** or starving. Some parts of the world are taking too much, while other parts have too little.

PROBLEM COWS?

There are about 1.5 billion cows in the world and they all release methane gas into the atmosphere when they belch and pass wind. A cow produces about the same pollution each day as one car.

There would be fewer cows in the world if there was less demand for **beef** as food. Raising cows also uses up a lot of water and land.

As the world warms up, **weather patterns** change. Places that had little rain are finding that they are being flooded.

There is only a limited amount of land on Earth for **growing food**. Scientists are always looking for new ways to grow foods that will produce enough to feed the world.

03 PEOPLE AND PLACES

There are more than 7 billion people living in the world today, in almost 200 countries. This number is growing fast. More than half of us live in cities and towns, but many people live in remote areas far from anywhere. Wherever we live, we have built many amazing places and found different ways to live together.

PEOPLE POWER

In 1800, the world's population was about 1 billion. By 1960, it had grown to 3 billion. Over the last 50 years, that figure has more than doubled. Some experts estimate that by 2050, there will be at least 9 billion people on the planet, and by 2100, perhaps more than 10 billion.

People need to work to earn money to feed themselves and their families. More and more people are choosing to live in towns and cities because there are more jobs there.

WHERE CAN WE LIVE?

Everyone needs somewhere safe and warm to live, but fitting everyone in is becoming more and more difficult. Our cities are becoming very crowded.

The United Nations declared 31st October 2011 **7 Billion Day**. On this date, the world's population reached 7 billion.

HAVING FUN!

People everywhere want to take time off from work and have fun with their family and friends. Soon it may be hard to find space to do this!

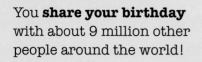

You **share your birthday** with about 9 million other people around the world!

Nearly half the world's population is under the **age of 25**.

GREAT AND SMALL

Vatican City is the smallest country in the world at only 0.5 sq km (0.2 sq miles). That is smaller than the average city! The largest country in the world is Russia, which is 17,075,400 sq km (6,592,846 sq miles).

CONTINENTAL COUNTRIES

The continent with the most countries is Africa, which has 54 countries. After Antarctica, South America has the fewest, with just 12.

China has a **population** of more than 1.36 billion. India is home to more than 1.26 billion people.

53

AFRICA

Although Africa has the most countries of any continent, many of its countries have the fewest people. In Libya, Botswana and Mauritania, for example, there are only three people per sq km (0.3 sq miles). It is a continent with an ancient history, and a wonderful variety of people living in lots of different ways.

The **Namib Desert** in Namibia, South Africa and Angola is the oldest desert in the world. It has been a desert for about 80 million years.

RECORD BREAKERS

The tallest and the fastest animals in the world live in Africa. The giraffe is the tallest and the cheetah is the fastest on land.

Africa is home to some of the largest **mammals** in the world and an amazing variety of wildlife.

The **Maasai** people are found in Tanzania and Kenya. They live by raising cattle. Part of their rituals involves piercing and stretching their earlobes!

Africa is where we all come from. It is where modern humans evolved about 200,000 years ago, before they spread across the world.

Victoria Falls on the Zambia-Zimbabwe border is one of the largest waterfalls in the world. It was given its name by an English explorer, David Livingstone. Its African name, 'Mosi-oa-Tunya', means 'the smoke that thunders'.

TALK TALK

More than 1,000 languages are spoken by the people of Africa.

Mount Kilimanjaro in Tanzania is the highest mountain in Africa, at 5,895 m (19,300 ft). Its top is permanently covered in ice.

Africa has produced some great **athletes**. Dennis Kimetto broke the world record for the marathon in 2014, taking the title from fellow Kenyan, Wilson Kipsang.

ASIA

Asia is by far the most populated continent, with more than 4 billion people. Many of Asia's cities are very crowded, but out in the countryside, life often carries on in the same way it has done for centuries.

The language spoken by the most people in the world is **Mandarin Chinese**. It is spoken by more than 1 billion people. This writing on the right-hand side says 'happy birthday' in Mandarin.

生日快樂

ANCIENT ART

The world's oldest art was found in a cave in Indonesia, southeast Asia. It dates back at least 40,000 years.

Singapore is one of the most crowded countries in the world, with 6,386 people living in every sq km (0.3 sq miles).

BOLLYWOOD

The Indian movie industry is known as Bollywood. It Is based in Mumbai and it Is one of the biggest film makers in the world. Billions of people watch Bollywood films.

THREE GORGES

The Three Gorges Dam in China is the world's largest hydroelectric power station. It uses water power from the Yangtze River to generate electricity.

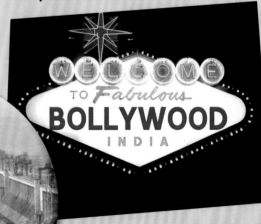
WELCOME TO *Fabulous* BOLLYWOOD INDIA

PEOPLE POWER

The two countries in the world with the highest number of people are in Asia (China and India). Both have more than 1 billion people.

DRAGONS!

There are real dragons in Asia! Komodo dragons live in Indonesia on Komodo Island and can be up to 3 m (10 ft) long. They like to eat deer.

The main food crop grown in Asia is rice. It grows in water, so it is suited to the climate. Rice seedlings are planted in the monsoon season.

Many areas of Asia have a period each year of very heavy rain called a **monsoon**. The monsoon season follows a long dry season, so the rains are usually welcome.

BRIGHT AND BEAUTIFUL

Diwali is the biggest and brightest festival in India. Many people, both in India and around the world, use this festival to celebrate the triumph of light over darkness.

ANTARCTICA

Antarctica is a difficult place to live. Almost all of its huge area is covered in ice and it is always freezing with a bitterly cold wind. However, people have been moving in over the last 100 years because there is so much to see and learn there. Scientists can learn about how our climate is changing by studying the melting ice.

The first people to spend a winter in Antarctica were **Belgians** who sailed there in 1897.

POOR SCOTT

British explorer Captain Robert F. Scott was desperate to be the first person to reach the South Pole. In December 1911, he was beaten to it by a Norwegian, Roald Amundsen. Scott and his party arrived at the Pole a month later, but they died on the way home.

00:00:02:12

Many countries have **research stations** in Antarctica. The biggest is the McMurdo Station, which the United States set up in 1956. Up to 1,000 people live there in summer.

Antarctica does not belong to any single country and it has no government. Several countries claim parts of it, but a treaty signed by 45 nations in 1959 agreed to keep the continent open for peaceful scientific study, with no military activity allowed.

The male **king penguin** keeps an unhatched egg warm on his feet, tucked under his fur all through the dark winter months, while the mother goes off to feed. When the female returns, the little chick has hatched.

KINGS OF THE ICE

Penguins live in the northern part of Antarctica. They can't fly and they waddle on land, but in the water they are fantastic swimmers. They live in large groups or colonies.

Tourists now visit Antarctica in the summer on cruise ships. They go to see the huge icy landscape, the penguins and the other wildlife.

DARK AND LIGHT

In winter in Antarctica, it is dark all day and night, but in summer it is light 24 hours a day.

GIFTS FROM SPACE

Antarctica is a good place for scientists to find out about meteorites (rocks that fall from space). They are easy to see on the white ice and they stay preserved in the cold.

EUROPE

More than 700 million people live in Europe. The landscape varies from frozen tundra and forests to high mountains and warm coasts. Europe is a crowded continent and people make their living in an extraordinary variety of ways. Europe's history makes it popular with tourists, who come to see the amazing buildings and traditions from the past.

Some of the countries of Europe have joined to form the **European Union**. They can trade freely between each other and their people can live in any of the member countries.

RELIGIOUS LEADER

The pope is the leader of the Roman Catholic Church. He lives in Vatican City, the world's smallest country, which is within Rome, Italy.

BIG SPORT

The largest attendance for a sporting event is the crowd of about 10 million people who gather over three weeks every year to watch Europe's Tour de France cycle race.

LONG AND THE SHORT

Europe has the world's longest place name, which is found in Wales. It is Llanfairpwllgwyngyll-gogerychwyrndrobwllllantysiliogogogoch, which means 'Saint Mary's Church in the hollow of the white hazel near a rapid whirlpool and the Church of St Tysilio of the red cave'. The shortest place name in Europe is in Sweden. It is Å, which means 'river'.

LLANFAIRPWLLGWYNGYLLGOGERYCHWYRNDROBWLLLLANTYSILIOGOGOGOCH

Å

Many **spruce** trees grow in northern European countries. The oldest living tree is a spruce tree in Sweden that has been growing for 9,550 years.

La Tomatina is a food fight festival held in August each year in the town of Buñol in Spain. Thousands of people make their way from all corners of the world to join 'the world's biggest food fight', where more than 90 tonnes (100 tons) of over-ripe tomatoes are thrown in the streets!

TALL DUTCH

The Dutch are the world's tallest citizens. Some people say that this is because they eat so much milk and cheese. Dutch men average 186 cm tall (6 ft 1 in) and women 172 cm (5 ft 7 in).

The Shard in London is the tallest building in the European Union. It is 309.6 m (1,016 ft) high and has 72 floors.

Queen Elizabeth II is the fortieth monarch to reign in England since William the Conqueror took the throne in 1066. She became queen in 1952.

61

NORTH AMERICA

North America consists of 23 countries, including the United States, Canada and Mexico. It has huge mountain ranges, grassy plains, deserts, tropical islands, beautiful beaches and rainforests. More than 500 million people live there, most of them in the large cities along the east and west coasts.

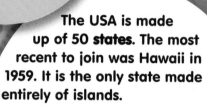

The USA is made up of 50 **states**. The most recent to join was Hawaii in 1959. It is the only state made entirely of islands.

A HUGE COUNTRY

Canada is close to 10 million sq km (4 million sq miles) in size. The United Kingdom could fit inside its borders 40 times over!

The first **Disneyland** opened in the United States in 1955. Walt Disney wanted to see how it was going, so he and his family lived in an apartment above the 'Fire Department' on Main Street.

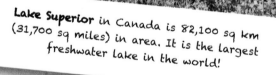

Lake Superior in Canada is 82,100 sq km (31,700 sq miles) in area. It is the largest freshwater lake in the world!

The **Empire State Building** in New York stands 103 floors high and was opened in 1931. It took just 1 year and 45 days to build! From the top you can see for 80 miles.

In **Mexico**, stone tools have been found that suggest humans were living there about 23,000 years ago.

Football is Mexico's most popular sport. The country has hosted the World Cup twice, in 1970 and 1986.

ROCKIN' ROCKIES

The Rocky Mountains in western North America are 76 million years old. Their highest peak is Mount Elbert in Colorado which is 4,401 m (14,440 ft). Most of the mountain range is protected as a national park.

FIRST FACTS

① The USA was the first country to send astronauts to the moon. Neil Armstrong was the first man to step onto the moon, in 1969.

② The first cartoon strip ever printed was 'The Yellow Kid', which first appeared in the *New York Journal* in October 1896!

I ♥ New York

SOUTH AMERICA

South America has the Pacific Ocean on one side and the Atlantic on the other. It has some extreme geographical features, such as the Andes Mountains and the immense Amazon River. It has a rich history and many different nationalities living in 12 countries.

The Amazon rainforest is the largest tropical rainforest in the world. It covers more than 5.5 million sq km (2 million sq miles). It flows through Brazil, Peru, Venezuela, Ecuador, Colombia, Guyana, Bolivia, Suriname and French Guiana.

The world's smallest monkey lives in the rainforest. The **pygmy marmoset**, or finger monkey, is only 13 cm (5 in) tall.

FLOATING FAMILIES

In Lake Titicaca, Peru, and Bolivia, the Uros people live on floating islands made out of woven reeds. They make their furniture out of reeds, too.

CARNIVAL TIME!

The world's biggest party takes place every year in Brazil. The Carnival marks the beginning of Lent, the 40-day period before Easter. Carnival lasts 5 days and huge, noisy parades march through the streets, with music and dancing.

Paraguay is in the middle of South America, with land on all sides. A kind of dance there called the 'gallopa' involves women balancing bottles on their heads as they dance.

One of Colombia's most popular snacks is roasted **ants**. The salted, roasted ants are eaten like peanuts.

GREAT GALÁPAGOS

The Galápagos Islands are in the Pacific Ocean off the coast of Ecuador. The islands are isolated, so many unique animal species live there, such as the Galápagos tortoise, Galápagos penguin and more than 50 species of fish.

Argentina is famous for rearing cattle. The cowboys there are called gauchos and they work on the grasslands, or pampas, herding cattle on horseback.

Robinson Crusoe is a story about a castaway stranded on a tropical island. It is based on the true story of a man who was shipwrecked off the coast of Chile.

Did you know?

The tomato is native to western South America. Today, tomatoes are grown in many countries around the world.

OCEANIA

The continent of Oceania includes Australia, New Zealand, Papua New Guinea and many islands in the South Pacific. In all these places, the native people have been joined by settlers who have moved from other parts of the world, to enjoy the fantastic scenery and weather.

SUPER SYDNEY

One in five Australians live in Sydney in the southeast. It is not the capital city, but it is by far the biggest.

EMPTY?

Large parts of Australia are empty. These areas are called the outback and are mainly desert. Most Australians live on the country's east coast.

There are more than 25,000 islands in Oceania.

GREAT BARRIER REEF

The Great Barrier Reef is a huge area of corals in the Coral Sea off the northeast coast of Australia. It covers the same area as Italy.

THE OLDEST RESIDENTS

Aborigines have been living in Australia for up to 125,000 years. They are well known for their beautiful art.

Uluru, the name of a famous massive sandstone rock in the Australian desert, is translated as 'great pebble'.

There are only two types of **egg-laying mammal**, the duck-billed platypus and the echidna, and both live only in Oceania.

RICHES

Australian mines produce almost 230 tonnes (254 tons) of gold per year. Australia is the second-largest gold producer, after China.

THE MAORI PEOPLE

① The Maori are the native people of New Zealand. They named their country 'Land of the long white cloud'.

② The New Zealand rugby team, the All Blacks, performs the Haka, a Maori war dance, before every match.

The two islands that make up **New Zealand** were formed by volcanoes millions of years ago. There are still many active volcanoes there.

67

EPIC JOURNEYS

Throughout history, people have wanted to explore the world. They have set out on dangerous journeys on foot, in boats and on horseback to find out more about the world around them.

Vasco da Gama was a Portuguese explorer. In 1947, he was the first person to sail directly from Europe to India, around the southern tip of Africa.

On a journey to cross Antarctica in 1915, British explorer **Ernest Shackleton's** ship sank and his crew was stranded. He took five men and set off to find help. They crossed 1,300 km (808 miles) of ocean, then walked across the ice until they found civilization.

Christopher Columbus sailed westwards from Spain in 1492, hoping to reach China and Japan. Instead, he found America in the way. Nobody in Europe knew it was there.

ROUND THE WORLD

In 1522, Portuguese explorer Ferdinand Magellan captained the first ship to sail all the way around the world. He proved that the world was round, when many people thought it was flat!

ON AND ON AND ON

The space probe *Voyager 1* was launched in 1977 and it is still going. It passed by Jupiter and Saturn before heading out to the edge of our solar system. It did not stop there. Scientists now think it is in interstellar space! It is the most distant human-made object ever.

Italy's **Marco Polo** wanted to know more about the Far East. He explored the trade routes to the East, called the Silk Road, and took 3 years to reach China.

New Zealand climber Edmund Hillary and his Nepalese guide Tenzing Norgay were the first people ever to reach the summit of **Mount Everest**, in May 1953.

CORTES IN MEXICO

In 1519, Hernán Cortés conquered the Aztec Empire in Mexico and claimed the land for Spain. Sadly, he took diseases to South America that people there had never experienced before. Thousands of native people died.

In 2012, **Felix Baumgartner**, an Austrian skydiver, broke the world record for the highest-ever skydive. He jumped from more than 39 km (24 miles) up in the stratosphere.

WONDERS OF THE PAST

Humans have been on Earth for thousands of years. We have built great towns and cities and we have invented amazing machines to make our lives easier, safer and more comfortable. Many of the wonders we created in the past can still be seen today.

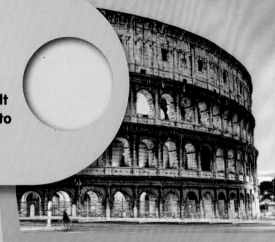

THE ROMANS

About 2,000 years ago, Rome in Italy was the capital of the Roman Empire, which stretched from Egypt to Britain. Some of the buildings built by the Romans are still standing, like the Colosseum in Rome.

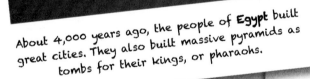

About 4,000 years ago, the people of **Egypt** built great cities. They also built massive pyramids as tombs for their kings, or pharaohs.

THE AZTECS

The Aztecs had one of the most advanced cultures in the Americas, with a large empire in the 1400s and 1500s. Their capital city was Tenochtitlan, which is now Mexico City. They built temples to worship their gods.

The city of **Petra** in Jordan was carved out of the red sandstone cliffs more than 2,000 years ago.

The **Great Wall of China** is the longest structure ever built, at about 6,000 km (3,700 miles) long. It was put up to defend the northern border of the country from invaders, from the 1300s to the 1600s.

CATHEDRAL CHURCHES

Many large Christian churches, called cathedrals, were built in Europe in medieval times. The cathedral in Chartres, France, is famous for its stunning stained glass windows. Many of them show stories from the life of Jesus.

00:00:02:

The **Statue of Liberty** stands on Liberty Island in New York, USA. It was a gift from France and it is a symbol of freedom.

The ancient Greeks built temples that are still standing today. Their style of architecture has been copied throughout history. **The Parthenon** in Athens was built for the Greek goddess Athena.

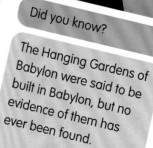

Did you know?

The Hanging Gardens of Babylon were said to be built in Babylon, but no evidence of them has ever been found.

71

HISTORY HEROES

There have been some truly incredible people who shaped the world in which they lived. Often, their influence has been felt long after they died. They may have invented something or ruled really well. Perhaps they created something beautiful or built up a huge empire. Whatever they did, they are today's history heroes.

Aristotle was a thinker and scientist born in 384 BCE in ancient Greece. He thought it was important to observe the world in order to understand it. This was the basis of modern science.

LEONARDO DA VINCI

Few people have been as multi-talented as the Italian Leonardo da Vinci. He lived from 1452 to 1519 and was an artist, scientist, engineer, mathematician, musician and writer.

The Tudors ruled England in the 1400s and 1500s. Henry VIII had six wives and his daughter Elizabeth I reigned for 44 years.

WALT DISNEY

Before he set up his film company, Walt Disney started a company called Laugh-O-Grams. It was a flop and he went bankrupt. He set off for Hollywood instead, with US $20 and one suitcase! The rest is history, as they say.

Spanish artist **Pablo Picasso** was one of the most famous artists of the twentieth century. His career lasted about 75 years and he created more than 13,000 paintings.

Abraham Lincoln was the sixteenth president of the United States. He is best remembered as the president who worked to end slavery in the United States.

DEFENDED IN DEATH

Chinese Emperor Qin Shi Huangdi was worried that he might be attacked after his death, so he ordered an army of warriors to be made in clay and buried with him. In just one pit, 7,000 soldiers and 600 horses have been found. Every warrior has been given a different face.

JULIUS CAESAR

① For a time, Julius Caesar was the most powerful man in the world. In 46 BCE, he became leader of the Roman Empire. He was appointed dictator for life and he ruled like a king.

② Caesar set up the Julian calendar, which we still use, with 365 days in a year and a leap year with 366 days.

③ In 44 BCE, he was killed by his enemies who thought he was too powerful.

HISTORY'S DISASTERS

Things have sometimes gone terribly wrong in the past. There have been conflicts and wars between peoples and countries. There have also been awful accidents and dreadful disasters.

The **Titanic** was a British passenger ship. It was supposed to be unsinkable, but on its first voyage, in 1912, it hit an iceberg and sank.

GREAT SMOG

In London, England, air was always full of smoke because people burned coal to heat their homes. In 1952, a mixture of car exhaust fumes and polluted winds from Europe made it almost impossible to see through the 'smog'. About 4,000 people died from breathing in this deadly air.

INDUSTRIAL DISASTER

The world's worst industrial disaster happened in 1984 when a poisonous gas leaked out of a chemical factory in Bhopal, India. More than 5,000 people and animals died from the poison and many more became sick.

The **Banqiao Dam** was built to control flooding in Henan province, China. It was supposed to be unbreakable but in 1975 it burst, affecting 11 million people.

Between 1845 and 1849 in **Ireland**, there was a Great Famine. Up to 1 million people died of hunger or disease.

The **First World War** of 1914–18 was the most disastrous war in history, in the number of lives lost. In all, 135 countries took part and more than 15 million people died.

TERRIBLE TAIPING

The Taiping Rebellion was a war between rebels and the rulers of China in 1850-64. The rebels disagreed with the way the ruling family was running the country. About 20 million people died and the rebels lost.

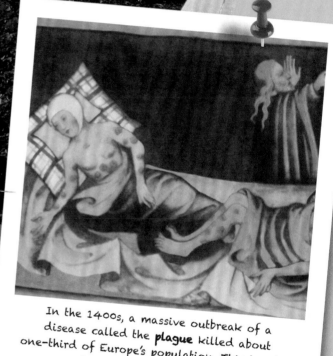

In the 1400s, a massive outbreak of a disease called the **plague** killed about one-third of Europe's population. This terrible event was called The Black Death.

In 1986, an explosion happened at a nuclear power plant in **Chernobyl**, Ukraine. Thousands of people became ill after coming into contact with the cloud, which spread over Europe.

04 ANIMALS AND PLANTS

We share Earth with many millions of other animals and plants. They live everywhere, from the bottom of the ocean to the top of the highest mountain. Some are huge and others are tiny. Some are striking, while others blend in to their surroundings. Some crawl, some fly, some can run like the wind. Together, they make a complex web of nature.

THE GIANTS

The biggest living things in the world are trees. Being big is not always easy. Large plants and animals have to support themselves. Big animals have to eat enough to survive and giant plants have to pull water through their stems all the way up to their leaves.

The **Goliath beetle** is about the size of your fist! It is the heaviest insect on Earth and weighs about the same as an apple.

The **giraffe** is the tallest land animal at an average height of 5 m (16 ft). It lives on the savannah of Africa and eats acacia tree leaves.

An adult female **blue whale** is the largest animal in the world. It is around half the length of an Olympic swimming pool. A baby blue whale weighs about the same as 600 cats!

FANTASTIC FRUIT
The fruits of the coco de mer palm tree can weigh up to 20 kg (44 pounds). They have the biggest seeds in the world.

WHAT A SQUEEZE!

Green anacondas are the heaviest snakes in the world. They can be more than 9 m (30 ft) long. That's nearly as long as a bus! They squeeze their prey to death in their powerful coils.

The **Siberian tiger** is the world's biggest cat. It is a deadly hunter and can eat 27 kg (60 pounds) of meat in one meal!

TALL TREES

The giant sequoia trees of California, United States, grow as high as skyscrapers with 20 floors or more. One, named General Sherman, is 84 m (275 ft) high! The biggest are thousands of years old.

UNDER THE SEA

(1) Giant clams are the biggest shellfish in the world. They can be 1 m (3 ft) across and live for 100 years.

(2) A great white shark can swallow a dolphin whole! These deadly hunters can grow to 8 m (26 ft) long. They have up to five rows of teeth and their jaws are incredibly powerful.

APES AND MONKEYS

Apes and monkeys are mammals. Mammals give birth to live young, rather than lay eggs, and feed their young on milk. Monkeys have tails, but apes do not. Apes are humans' closest relatives in the animal kingdom.

The **orangutan** is an ape. It is the largest animal that lives mainly in trees. It has very strong arms to hold on tight to branches and a large brain. It lives in the forests of Borneo and Sumatra in Asia.

The **spider monkey** is incredibly good at swinging through the trees. Its curly tail grips the branches like an extra hand.

QUIET UP THERE!

The guenon monkey lives in Africa, up in the trees. It likes to shout! It stuffs its cheek pouches with food, to keep for later when it finds a safe place to eat.

One of the largest monkeys in the world is the **baboon**. It is clever and lives in groups on the ground. To scare hunters, baboons show their teeth and chatter!

Chimpanzees are very clever apes. They can 'talk' to each other by making sounds and pulling faces. They usually walk on all fours, but they can also stand up and shuffle along on two legs.

Monkeys spend hours every day **grooming** each other. They pick bugs, seeds and twigs out of their fur.

GREAT GORILLA

Gorillas are the 'big daddies' of the ape world. They are found in central Africa and can live for up to 40 years. Each group is led by a male silverback, who beats his chest to chase away attackers.

00:00:02:12

Lemurs are relatives of monkeys. They live only on the island of Madagascar, off the east coast of Africa. They live in trees in family groups.

One of the rarest monkeys in the world is the **golden lion tamarin** of South America. Tamarins have a 'mane' and a long golden tail. They are endangered because their forest home is being cut down.

FROGS AND SNAKES

Frogs and toads are amphibians, with smooth skin. Most amphibians can live on land and in the water. They go to the water to mate and lay their eggs. Reptiles usually live on land. Snakes are reptiles and have scaly skin. They kill either by injecting their prey with poison or by squeezing it to death.

SLITHERING SNAKES

① Snakes cannot bite their food, so they have to swallow it whole. Their jaws are incredibly flexible and they can fit in creatures bigger than their head! This one is eating a lizard!

② Snakes live on every continent except Antarctica and there are about 3,000 different kinds. They smell with their tongues.

RATTLE ATTACK

Rattlesnakes have a 'rattle' of old scales at the end of their bodies. They shake them as if to say, 'Keep away or I will bite you!'

The **pit viper** has a bag of poison under the skin on each side of its head. Holes under its eyes detect heat given off by the warm bodies of its prey.

SUPER SIGHT

Frogs can see forwards, sideways and upwards all at once! They never shut their eyes, even when they are asleep.

LONG JUMP!

Frogs can jump more than six times their own length in one leap!

Frogs have nostrils, but they also take in air through their skin.

Frogs **croak** by pushing air through their throat. Most have a sac of skin that swells to make the sound louder.

BIG TOAD

Toads have warty skin and shorter legs than frogs. The cane toad is bigger than an adult's hand. It catches insects and worms with its sticky tongue.

It takes 3 weeks for a **tadpole** to grow into an adult frog.

BEAUTIFUL BIRDS

Birds are the only animals with feathers, but not all birds can fly. Ostriches are the largest birds, but they can only walk or run, while penguins use their wings for swimming. Birds come in a magnificent variety of shapes and sizes and are often stunningly beautiful.

Birds have hollow **bones**, which makes them lighter. This means it is easier for them to fly.

SO MANY BIRDS

One-fifth of all the bird species in the world live in the Amazon rainforest in South America.

Hummingbirds are the only birds that can fly backwards.

European **swallows** make an epic journey every year. At the end of summer, they set off for South Africa or Arabia! They fly 322 km (200 miles) a day, every day. They turn around and fly back to Europe in the spring.

The **kiwi** of New Zealand lays the biggest eggs of any bird relative to the size of its body. These birds live in burrows in the ground and come out to eat at night.

The **peregrine falcon** is the fastest animal in the whole world. When it dives to catch a bird, it flies as fast as 320 kph (200 mph).

FRUIT PICKERS

Toucans live in the rainforest but they cannot fly very well. They use their huge beaks to pick fruit from the trees.

Oxpeckers live on other animals. They eat all the little insects that burrow into the animals' fur and skin, so their hosts are delighted to have them!

PRETTY IN PINK

Flamingoes live in flocks beside water sources, such as lakes. The small, pink bacteria they eat in the water, makes them pink, too! No one knows why they like to stand on one leg.

The **eagle owl** is one of the biggest owls in the world. It is strong enough to attack animals like hares and ducks with its needle-sharp claws.

DINOSAURS

No one has ever seen a living dinosaur. The last dinosaurs died out about 65 million years ago. However, we have found fossils of their bones and teeth and even their footprints. So we have a pretty good idea of what these creatures were like. Some were huge, others were smaller but incredibly speedy.

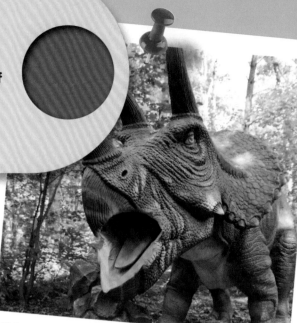

Triceratops was rather like a huge rhinoceros. It had three horns on its face, which it used to fight its enemies, such as Tyrannosaurus rex.

TERROR ON LEGS

The Tyrannosaurus rex had sharp teeth as long as bananas and jaws strong enough to crush bones. It weighed more than an elephant.

THIEF!

The Oviraptor's name means 'egg thief'. It stole eggs, then used the sharp spikes in its mouth to break them open to eat.

EXTRAORDINARY EGGS

Many dinosaurs hatched out of eggs. About 10–30 eggs were laid at a time in a nest on the ground.

One of the fastest dinosaurs was **Hypsilophodon**. It lived in groups and it could run very fast if it spotted danger.

Some dinosaurs lived in the water. The **Plesiosaur** lived in the sea and ate fish.

LARGEST FLIERS

The biggest creatures ever to fly were the pterosaurs that flew above the dinosaurs. Their wings were made of strong skin joined to a long 'finger'.

The body of a **Stegosaurus** was 500 times bigger than its brain, which was the size of a walnut! Its sharp spiky tail could deal a deadly blow.

The **Pachycephalosaurus** has been nicknamed 'bonehead' because of its thick, bony crash helmet. It used this in head-butting contests with its enemies.

CREEPY CRAWLIES

About 90 per cent of all the animals on Earth are insects and other minibeasts. All insects have six legs and three parts to their bodies. Spiders have eight legs and snails have just one, squishy foot.

INSECT SOCIETY

Some insects, such as bees, termites and ants, live in well-structured social groups. Termite mounds can be up to 12 m (40 ft) tall, which is as high as a three-storey building. They are home to thousands of termites.

Tarantulas can survive for up to 2.5 years without food. Their bodies are big and hairy, but their poison is actually weaker than that of a honeybee.

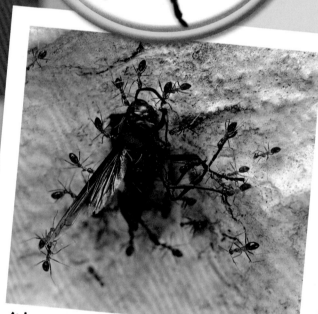

Ants can lift at least 20 times their own weight. They often work together to lift bigger objects. There are more than 20,000 different kinds of ant.

Dung beetles eat animal waste. They especially love the dung of plant eaters. They even lay their eggs in it.

The **giant weta ant** is the world's largest insect. It is an amazing 10 cm (4 in) long.

LOOKING BACKWARDS

The praying mantis is the only insect that can turn its head to look backwards, so you cannot sneak up on one. The female mantis sometimes eats the male after they have mated.

The **cricket** has huge back legs so it can jump a long way. It has 'ears' on its front legs to detect sounds.

DEADLY SCORPIONS

Scorpions are arachnids, like spiders. They have pincers at the front for fighting. The deadly part is the tail with a sting on the end. The pincers at the front are for fighting.

HEADLESS ROACH

The brain of a cockroach is in its body, so even if it lost its head, it could survive for days before dying of hunger.

FLYING INSECTS

Sometimes, they are annoying when they buzz around you, or even worse sting you, but flying insects are some of the most awesome creatures on Earth. Many of them play an important part in our lives.

Only female **wasps** can sting because the sting is made from an egg-laying tool. They can take their poisonous sting out of a victim and use it again.

Honeybees can fly at about 25 kph (15 mph) and beat their wings 200 times per second.

FLIES IN THE SUGAR?

Houseflies taste with their feet. Their tongues are 10 million times more sensitive to sugar than ours are.

BRILLIANT BEES

We need bees to pollinate flowers, fruits and vegetables. This makes it possible for the plants to grow seeds and fruit.

Dragonflies have six legs, but they cannot walk. They can fly incredibly fast, though, at around 30-60 kph (18-37 mph). They use their legs to scoop up gnats to eat.

DISEASE CARRIERS

Female mosquitoes carry a deadly disease called malaria. They pass malaria on to humans when they bite us to suck our blood.

Tarantula wasps stun tarantula spiders, then lay a single egg on them. When the egg hatches, the wasp larva feeds on the living spider.

Queen Alexandra's birdwing butterfly has a wingspan of more than 28 cm (11 in). It lives in Papua New Guinea.

The **desert locust** is the world's most destructive insect. It can eat its own body weight of food in a day. Swarms of locusts can quickly destroy fields of crops.

SCARY AND SNEAKY

There are some animals that have amazing disguises and super survival techniques. There are other animals that you have to keep well away from. They may be clever, but they can also be deadly. Make sure you know which they are.

Fleas are insects that live off other animals. They survive by sucking their prey's blood.

GOODNIGHT?

Mites like to live in warm, dark, moist places like your bed. They eat flakes of dead skin. Your mattress may contain plenty of mites, but they are too tiny to see.

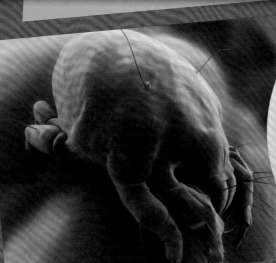

Female flower spiders can change their appearance to match the flowers they hide on, while they wait for their prey.

VENOMOUS VICTOR

The most poisonous spiders in the world are Brazilian wandering spiders. They hide in the rainforest by day and come out at night when you cannot see them.

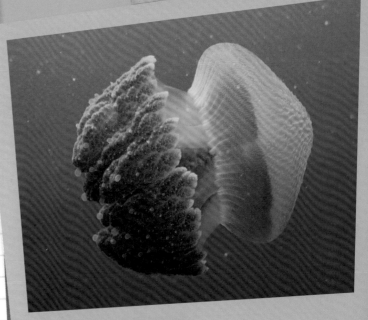

DEADLY STING

Beware of the box jellyfish! Its tentacles can sting a person to death in under 5 minutes. They are found off the coast of Australia.

A **vampire bat** drinks about two teaspoons of blood each day. Its fangs sink into its prey.

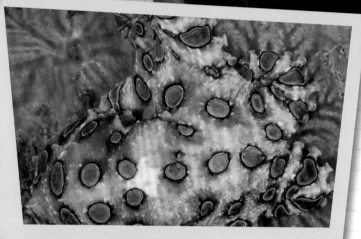

BLUE STINGERS

The blue-ringed octopus is tiny, but its spit is so poisonous, it can stun up to ten people in one go. It usually uses its poison to kill crabs.

BRILLIANT DISGUISE

The leafy sea dragon grows fake seaweed all over its body, so that it cannot be seen by hunters.

The **cuttlefish** has a great escape technique. When it is attacked, it squirts out clouds of black ink. This gives it time to swim away.

93

ANIMAL OLYMPICS

The incredible variety of animals on Earth includes many record-breaking creatures. They can run, swim and fly amazingly fast. They can be hugely strong, too. These are just a few of the creatures that are definitely champions in the animal Olympics.

The blue marlin fish can swim more than ten times faster than an Olympic champion.

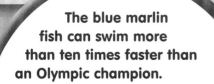

THAT'S AMAZING!

An octopus can squeeze through an opening no bigger than the size of its own eyeball.

The fastest shark in the sea is the **shortfin mako**. If a shark stops swimming, though, it sinks, so it never stops moving.

CLEAN GIRAFFES

A giraffe can clean its own ears with its 50 cm (21 in) tongue. It can also last longer without water than a camel.

Grizzly bears can run after their prey faster than an Olympic sprinter.

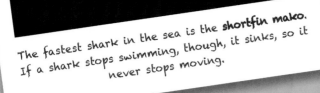

The fastest swimming bird is the **gentoo penguin,** which can hit bursts of 35 kph (26 mph).

Elephants can run up to 40 kph (25 mph) but they cannot jump.

The **crocodile** has the greatest bite force ever measured in a living animal, but the muscles that open the jaw are so weak, they can be kept shut using a rubber band.

HEAVY FISH

The heaviest bony fish in the ocean is the sunfish, which has been recorded weighing 2 tonnes (2.2 tons).

Lions roar to scare off other lions that stray onto their territory. A lion's roar can be heard up to 10 km (6 miles) away.

PLANT POWER

We are surrounded by plants. Even if you live in the middle of a big city, there is a plant somewhere near you. Plants make their food from sunlight combined with carbon dioxide in the air, in a process called photosynthesis. Their roots take in water and nutrients and their leaves catch the sunlight. There are hundreds of thousands of different plants in the world.

STINKY GIANT

The largest flower in the world is the *titan arum*. It produces flowers 2.5 m (8 ft) tall and 1 m (3 ft) wide. The flowers smell really horrible, so they are also known as corpse flowers.

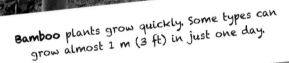

Bamboo plants grow quickly. Some types can grow almost 1 m (3 ft) in just one day.

In the Netherlands in the 1600s, **tulip bulbs** were more valuable than gold.

FLOWERS AND FORESTS

① In the past, the juice from bluebell flowers was used to make glue.

② About one-third of the United States is covered by forests.

Vanilla comes from the vanilla pod, which is actually the fruit of a kind of orchid flower.

WE LOVE PLANTS

Plants are an essential part of our diet. We use grains to make bread, rice and pasta. We eat fruit and vegetables of all kinds and we use herbs to make our food tasty.

Lots of plants are used to make **medicines**. The painkiller aspirin originally came from the bark of the willow tree.

Another very important thing plants have given us is **wood**. Think how many things around us are made from it.

Every plant has its own design of **pollen**. Some pollen grains have grooves, others have spikes. Some are light enough to be blown by the wind, others are sticky and carried by animals.

FLOWERS FOREVER

Inside a flower, male pollen grains are carried to the female parts of the flower, often by insects. Seeds develop inside the flower, which can then die away. Before that happens, though, the flowers give us the most amazing show of their beauty. They often have heavenly scents, too.

Most plants grow **flowers** each year, but some take much longer. The century plant, or agave, grows only one flower after many years and then it dies.

The **rosy periwinkle** lives in the rapidly disappearing rainforests on the island of Madagascar.

TEENY TINY

The smallest flowering plant in the world is thought to be the common watermeal. Its leaves are only 1 mm (0.04 in) across.

KEEP THE CYCADS

Cycads have lived on Earth since the days of the dinosaurs, but today, they are in real danger of dying out. They have a thick trunk and a crown of leaves.

Lithops grow in very dry conditions. To avoid being eaten by animals, the plants look just like stones.

The giant white flower of the **Amazon water lily** is the size of a football. The flower turns purple after it has been pollinated.

REALLY, ROSES?

Rose plants are related to apples, raspberries, cherries, peaches, plums, nectarines, pears and almonds.

HEAD TURNERS

Sunflowers turn their heads through the day in response to the movement of the sun across the sky, from east to west.

The **scents** of plants usually come from oils in the flowers. These can be removed and used to make perfumes. Some perfumes are a mixture of 50 different smells.

PECULIAR PLANTS

Most of the plants around us seem quite ordinary, but there are some truly weird plants in the world. Often, they have become like that to survive in the difficult places they inhabit. Some of them just look extreme, but others can do us serious harm.

Puya plants grow in the mountains of South America. Their stalks can be 4 m (13 ft) high. They take about 150 years to flower and then they die.

VENUS FLYTRAP

Some plants, such as the Venus flytrap, are carnivores (meat eaters). They trap insects and once these have died and decomposed, they feed off the nutrients left behind.

The **European edelweiss** is found on mountains. Its flowers are covered with hairs to protect them from the sun and wind.

Moon flowers bloom only at night. They close during the day.

The **silver torch cactus** is woolly. Its red flowers grow out straight from its sides and it really likes the cold. It can stand temperatures as low as -10 °C (14 F). It lives in the high mountains of Bolivia and Argentina and in winter it gets almost no water at all.

STINKY SKUNK

The skunk cabbage grows in the swamps of North America. It has huge golden flowers, it looks like an alien and it stinks. It is poisonous if you eat it, too.

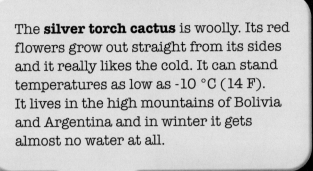

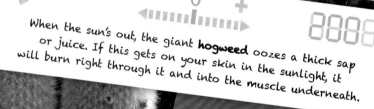

When the sun's out, the giant **hogweed** oozes a thick sap or juice. If this gets on your skin in the sunlight, it will burn right through it and into the muscle underneath.

At certain times of year, sea water at the beach can turn a rusty red. This is because thousands of tiny seaweeds, called algae, multiply into a huge carpet of plants. This algae kills fish and birds and is poisonous to us, too. This scary is called a **red tide**.

CLOSED
TO SHELLFISHING
RED TIDE

05

HOW WE LIVE

The world's population is growing, but not everyone lives in crowded places. Some people live in small communities in the countryside. They farm the land to grow food. Other people live in the forests or the mountains. Wherever people live, they all need the same basic things, like food, shelter, a family and friends. They find these things in many different ways.

SUPER CITIES

We like living together. People move into cities to find work so they can earn money to feed themselves and their families. Throughout history, we have built some beautiful cities around the world. Today, as the world's population is growing so fast, our cities are getting bigger and more crowded. We need more space to find a place for everyone to live well.

The city with the most people is **Tokyo**, the capital city of Japan. More than 37 million people live there.

CAPITAL CITIES

Each country has a capital city. It is usually, but not always, the biggest city in that country. The capital of Australia is Canberra, but far more people live in Sydney.

Dubai in the United Arab Emirates has been created very fast. In 1975, just 183,000 people lived there. Today, there are more than 2 million.

NEW YORK

The city of New York contains some of the most famous skyscrapers in the world, such as the Empire State Building and the Chrysler Building. They stand on the island of Manhattan.

London, England, was built over centuries. It contains many signs of the past, in its old streets and buildings.

Modern **Rome** is full of the ruins of ancient buildings, which millions of tourists go to see.

CITY LIVING

In Brazil, about three-quarters of the population live in cities. The largest city, Sao Paulo, has more than 11 million people living there.

TERRIBLE CONDITIONS

In poor countries, slums may grow up around the outsides of the biggest cities. The living conditions here are dreadful, people live in shacks and have no clean water or toilets. Kibera, on the outskirts of Nairobi in Kenya, is Africa's biggest slum.

The City of London is a 'city' within England's capital. Statues of dragons mark its boundaries.

105

AMAZING HOMES

Houses are made of a multitude of materials and come in many shapes and sizes. They are usually designed to suit their location, for example, to keep out the cold, the heat or the rain. As a result of this, they look very different in different parts of the world.

High-rise **apartment** buildings are built in places where land is in short supply, such as Hong Kong, or where land is very expensive, such as London or New York City.

MAASAI HOUSES

In East Africa, the Maasai live in homes built by the women. They weave a frame of branches and cover it with mud, grass and dung. This suits them because they travel across the land and can build new homes as they go.

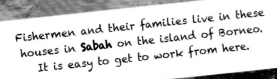

Fishermen and their families live in these houses in **Sabah** on the island of Borneo. It is easy to get to work from here.

These houses in **Scotland** were built more than 100 years ago from blocks of stone. The stone came from local rocks. The roofs are made of slate, another kind of local stone.

In **Yemen** in the Middle East, people built homes with many levels hundreds of years before skyscrapers were invented. Each floor of the house had its own purpose, such as for visitors or for women only.

The **Inuit** people who live in the Arctic build igloos from blocks of ice. They shelter in their igloos during hunting trips. It is surprisingly warm and cosy inside.

YURTS FOR MONGOLS

In Mongolia, Asia, the Mongols live in yurts. This is a wooden frame covered in pads of felt made from sheep's wool. Families need a movable house because they travel from place to place with herds of animals.

In **Tunisia**, North Africa, to beat the heat, some people live in underground homes carved out of the rock. A pit is dug in the ground, then caves are cut out of the sides to make homes.

In the countries of **Scandinavia** in northern Europe, homes are often built of wood, because the towns and villages are surrounded by forests of trees.

WORKING HARD

What job would you like to do when you're older? There are thousands to choose from. People work to provide shelter and food for their families. Some grow their own food. Most people work for money to buy the things they need. Around the world, there are some jobs that definitely seem weirder than others.

TOY TESTER

Someone has to dream up the new ideas for makers of toys. Toy companies employ people to design and test new products.

Some people work in jobs where they grow or find the **food** that other people buy. Farmers grow food, while fishermen go to sea in boats to catch fish.

DANGER!

Some jobs are dangerous. For example, **firefighters** turn up when there is a fire, to help keep other people safe.

HELPING US

Some people work in jobs where they help other people. Doctors and nurses look after our health. Bus and train drivers get us to where we want to go. Shop assistants help us find what we are looking for.

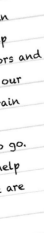

MAKING IT

Some people like to make things. They may be skilled at a craft that they do by hand, such as pottery, or work in a factory with big machines.

DREAM JOB

Some people are paid to go to sleep. They work for hotels and have to test out how comfortable it is to sleep in their rooms at night. Nice work if you can get it.

Only a few people get to be **astronauts**, but if you are one of the lucky ones, it is a job that is out of this world.

There are many jobs that **entertain** us. Some people take to the stage or are in films, other people do things that are just plain crazy.

FOOD SCIENTIST

Ever thought of being a food scientist? If you are lucky, you might get the job of tasting new types of ice cream for the manufacturer.

AWESOME ACHIEVEMENTS

Humans have achieved some truly awesome things. We have found out so much about science and created beautiful works of art and music. We have developed laws that control our behaviour and invented new technologies. Some of the things we have achieved, though, are a bit more random.

Some people do difficult things just for the fun of it. **Bob Blumer** of Canada made a record-breaking 559 pancakes in one hour, in a competition in 2008. Hopefully, he did not have to eat them all.

A POLAR ACHIEVEMENT

Skiing to the North and South Poles is hard enough when you are young and fit. A German man named Norbert Kern skied to the South Pole in January 2007, then to the North Pole just 3 months later. He was 66 years old at the time.

The record for the most **babies** born to one woman is 69. Included in this total were 16 pairs of twins, seven sets of triplets and four sets of quadruplets.

In 2006, **Dee Caffari** sailed around the world westwards. Then in 2009, she sailed around the world eastwards, making her the first woman to sail around the world in both directions.

The **Palm Jumeirah** in Dubai is the world's largest man-made island. It is even visible from space. It opened in 2006.

UP AND UP

It took Italian Reinhold Messner 16 years to complete his achievement of climbing every mountain in the world higher than 8,000 m (26, 246 ft). There are 14 of these mega mountains.

The **Atlantic Ocean** is huge, but in 2008, a crew of 14 British and Irish men rowed across it. It took them 33 days, 7 hours and 30 minutes.

SUPER RICH

Some people who have achieved enormous wealth have also been generous in their donations to good causes. Bill and Melinda Gates, for example, have given away more than US $30 billion so far.

Did you know?

The first person ever to run a mile in less than four minutes was English athlete Roger Bannister. In Oxford in 1954, he ran a mile in 3 minutes 59.4 seconds.

SUPER SPORTS

There are hundreds of sports to choose from. Some you can play as an individual, like tennis. Others you play in a team. Playing sport is a fantastic way to stay fit and share a good time with others. Some people make sport their career and have a lot of success, and millions of spectators love to watch them.

Golf is the only sport that has been played on the moon. On 6 February 1971, astronaut Alan Shepard hit a golf ball there.

FABULOUS FOOTBALL

Association football, or soccer, is the most attended and watched sport in the world.

The **high jump** method of jumping head-first and landing on your back is called the Fosbury Flop.

Manchester United is the United Kingdom's most successful football team. They have won 35 major home trophies. The second best team is Liverpool, with 33 major home trophies.

A **baseball ball** has exactly 108 stitches and a cricket ball has between 65 and 70 stitches.

AN OLD COMPETITION

The oldest continuous trophy in sport is the America's Cup, a sailing race. It started in 1851 and the United States won it for 132 years in a row, until Australia took the Cup in 1983. It was the longest winning streak in history.

Golf was banned in England in 1457 because it was thought to be a distraction from the more worthwhile sport of archery.

FIRST FORMULA ONE

Ferenc Szisz from Romania won the first ever Formula One Grand Prix, driving a Renault. The race was held at Le Mans, France, in 1906.

TENNIS, ANYONE?

① Each year, about 42,000 tennis balls are used in the Wimbledon Championships in London, England, in about 650 matches.

② The fastest serve ever recorded in tennis was by Samuel Groth from Australia. In 2012, he served the ball at 263.4 kph (163.7 mph). The fastest women's serve was from Sabine Lisicki of Germany. In 2014, she hit a serve of 210.8 kph (131 mph). Their poor opponents!

113

GLOBAL COMPETITIONS

The Olympic Games and the FIFA World Cup are two of the biggest sporting events in the world. Both are held every four years, and they attract hundreds of millions of viewers on television. The countries of the world come together, either in teams or as individuals, to do their very best and show just what humans are capable of.

Olympic **gold** medals are actually made of silver and are coated with gold. The bronze medals are mostly made of copper.

FIRST OLYMPICS

The Olympic Games were first held in Olympia, ancient Greece. The first Olympic race, held in 776 BCE, was won by Coroebus, who was a chef.

The United States has won more medals at the **Olympic Games** than any other country.

SUMMER AND WINTER

The Winter Olympics take place two years after the Summer Olympics. They include winter sports such as skiing and ice hockey.

Great Britain's most decorated Olympian is cyclist Chris Hoy. At London's 2012 Olympic Games, he won his fifth and sixth gold medals.

The five **Olympic rings** represent the five major regions of the world (Africa, the Americas, Asia, Europe and Oceania). Every national flag in the world has a shade matching at least one of the five rings.

The base of the current FIFA **World Cup** trophy has space for 17 inscriptions. This is enough for every winner until 2038.

IMPRESSIVE TOTAL

At the 2008 Games in Beijing, China, swimmer Michael Phelps won eight gold medals for the United States. This is the most ever won by a single competitor in one Olympic competition. In his Olympic career so far, Phelps has won 18 gold medals.

The first ever **World Cup** match was played in 1930 and won by the host nation, Uruguay. They beat Argentina 4-2 in the final.

Brazil is the most successful national football team in the history of the World Cup. They have won the competition five times!

In 1958, Brazilian football legend **Pelé** was 17 years old when he became the youngest player ever to score a goal at the World Cup.

MAKING MUSIC

Around the world, people make music in a great variety of ways. Music is always intended to be performed, or listened to. It can be written down in advance or just played on the spot. It can be sung with your voice or played on instruments. You can make music alone or with others. Music is a fantastic way to express yourself and have fun!

EARLY MUSIC

The earliest instruments we have found are up to 40,000 years old! They are tubes of wood, bone or ivory with holes drilled into them, like a recorder or flute.

CHINESE MUSIC

Many Chinese instruments have a very long history. The guzheng is a stringed instrument like a zither that is plucked.

The **harmonica** is the world's best-selling musical instrument. To play it, the musician blows through the holes on its side.

WRITE IT DOWN

The oldest piece of written music ever found is from 408 BCE. The music was from an ancient Greek play called Orestes, which was written by Euripides.

The Indian **sitar** has strings and a long, hollow neck. It is played by being plucked.

After the release of their album *Four* in 2014, **One Direction** became the first band in the United States ever to have their first four albums enter the charts at number one.

BAGPIPES

The bagpipes were not invented by the Scottish, but by the ancient Romans in the first century CE.

BEST BEATLES

The best-selling pop band in history is The Beatles, with sales of more than 600 million records worldwide. They were together from 1960 to 1970.

Music can be downloaded from the Internet. In 2014, the UK's most downloaded song was 'Happy' by **Pharrell Williams**. By September, it had been downloaded 1.62 million times!

CREATIVE AND CURIOUS

People have been making art for many thousands of years. Ancient artists were judged by their skill, for example in painting or pottery, not for their creative ideas. Today art is big business for some, but anyone can make wonderful art if they just have a go!

In Africa, people often made **masks** out of wood. They were usually made to be used in religious ceremonies.

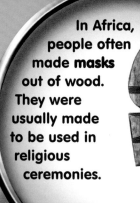

MONKS AT WORK

Before printing was invented, monks in Europe made books by hand. They wrote out the words and drew detailed illustrations. They were not thought of as artists, but their work was certainly beautiful.

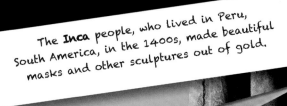

The **Inca** people, who lived in Peru, South America, in the 1400s, made beautiful masks and other sculptures out of gold.

SLOW TO SMILE

Leonardo da Vinci spent four years painting the Mona Lisa, from 1503 to 1507, and it was still not finished until years later! It is one of the most viewed paintings in the world.

Sculpture has often been used to decorate buildings. In many different civilizations of the past, religious buildings were richly decorated with carvings. These carvings are from a Hindu temple at Ellora in India.

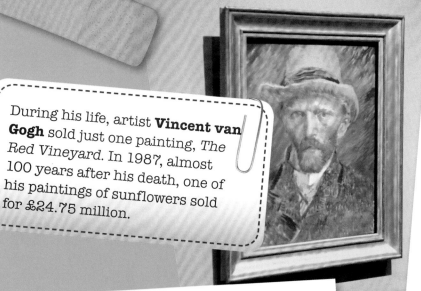

During his life, artist **Vincent van Gogh** sold just one painting, The Red Vineyard. In 1987, almost 100 years after his death, one of his paintings of sunflowers sold for £24.75 million.

The first **pencil** was invented in England in 1565, after a huge amount of graphite was discovered underground in Cumbria.

Art does not have to be shown in a **gallery**. Some artists make art to be displayed outside, like sculptures, or even paint their art on the sides of buildings!

CHINA IN CHINA

The Chinese were the best in the world at making beautiful objects out of a thin kind of china called porcelain. They painted their vases and bowls with elaborate patterns. Dragons were a sign of power and strength.

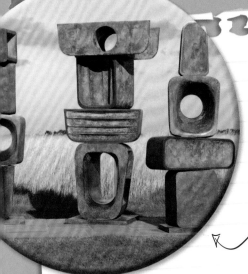

Art does not have to look like something we know. This sculpture by English artist Barbara Hepworth, made in 1970, is called 'The Family of Man'.

MONEY

Money is what we use to pay for the things we need and want, such as good or services, or to pay bills and debts. Money is also one way of counting the value of something. Most countries of the world have their own kind of money, called currency. The government prints the money that everyone uses.

The makers of the board game **Monopoly** print more than $50 billion worth of Monopoly money every year.

EXPENSIVE TO BUILD

The most expensive object ever built is the International Space Station, which has so far cost around US$150 billion!

PAPER MONEY

① The world's first paper money was invented in China 1,400 years ago.

② Banknotes are made of cotton and linen, not paper, to make them stronger.

The first city to make its own **gold coins** was Florence, Italy, in 1252. They were called 'florins'.

The **flu virus** can live on banknotes for more than 2 weeks, and it can pass from person to person.

The island of **Yap** in Micronesia uses huge stone disks, called Rai, as their currency. Some Rai weigh up to 4 tonnes (4.4 tons).

BIG MONEY

The largest banknote ever issued by the Bank of England was for £1 million and was issued in 1948.

Queen Elizabeth II has appeared on the currencies of 33 countries. This banknote is from the Bahamas.

The most valuable company in the world is **Apple**, the makers of the iPhone.

In Zimbabwe in 2008, a loaf of bread cost 10 million Zimbabwe dollars due to **inflation**, which means money has less value than previously.

FAME AND FORTUNE

All through history, some people have become especially well-known in the places where they lived. Perhaps they wrote wonderful stories, made great works of art, or invented something useful. In our modern world, we can find out about what famous people are doing anywhere! A person's fame can be global.

Nelson Mandela was a South African politician, who died in 2013. He went to prison for 27 years for protesting against his country's government. He later became president of South Africa and worked hard for peace and equality.

KING OF FRANCE

King Louis XIV of France ruled his country from 1643–1715. He made sure everyone knew how rich and powerful he was by transforming the vast palace near Paris, called Versailles.

DAVID BECKHAM

Sports stars are some of the most famous people in the world today. British footballer David Beckham, retired from the sport in 2013, but people still follow his life and work.

The young stars of the *Harry Potter* movies were paid millions of pounds to star in those films and they became hugely famous.

Hollywood in California, United States, is home to many stars. Celebrities, such as Angelina Jolie and Brad Pitt, are followed by fans wherever they go.

There are about 1,800 people in the world today who are worth more than **US$1 billion**.

WITHOUT A FORTUNE

Mohandas 'Mahatma' Gandhi was born in India in 1869. He became famous, but he never had a fortune. Gandhi campaigned for India's independence from the British Empire. He believed in non-violent protest and his work encouraged others around the world. He died in 1948.

GATES OF GOLD

The richest man in the world is Bill Gates. He started up the computer company Microsoft. His worth is estimated to be more than US$80 billion.

Lewis Hamilton became the youngest person ever to win the Formula One World Championship in 2008, aged just 23. He won it again in 2014. He is Britain's richest sports star.

WAR AND WEAPONS

Ever since people began to settle in communities thousands of years ago, they have fought with other communities. Sometimes, these fights grow so big that they become wars. People have invented some truly terrible ways of fighting their enemies, with weapons to use on land, in the sea and in the air.

The Aztecs, who lived in Mexico in the 1400s, fought with a **maquahuitl**. This was a wooden staff studded with very sharp blades made of glass.

SECOND WORLD WAR

The Second World War lasted 6 years, from 1939 to 1945. Most of the world's countries fought on one side or the other; the Allies or the Axis. Millions of people died and cities all over the world were destroyed by bombs. The Allies won the war in the end.

The **Battle of Agincourt** was fought in 1415 between the English and French, in the Hundred Years' War. Here, people are re-enacting King Henry V's army's victory.

The **Spitfire** was an important British fighter plane of the Second World War. It had an amazing top speed of 720 kph (447 mph) and was armed with up to eight machine guns.

In the first **cannons**, gunpowder was put at the back of a huge metal tube and a cannonball was placed at the front. When the gunpowder was lit, it exploded and the cannonball shot out of the top at a great speed.

Both **gunpowder** and **cannons** were invented by the Chinese.

The first **nuclear weapon** to be used was a bomb dropped by the United States on the Japanese city of Hiroshima on 6 August 1945. This led to the end of the Second World War.

STEALTH BOMBER

Stealth planes seem to appear out of nowhere. They can slip through air space undetected because they are covered in a special paint that hides them from radar.

Submarines travel underwater through the oceans. They carry missiles that can be fired at enemy ships to sink them.

06 FANTASTIC FOOD

We have to eat to stay alive! Around the world, people eat the foods that grow well where they live. Today, planes can fly foods from anywhere in the world to anywhere else, but many people still enjoy their own country's dishes. Some of the things people enjoy eating may seem a bit odd to others, or even off-putting!

EAT TO LIVE

The foods you eat make up your diet. A healthy diet contains foods of several different kinds, called food groups. These groups go well together and they support your body in different ways. You need to eat more foods from some groups than others.

The average person in a rich country will consume 100 tonnes (110 tons) of **food** and 45,424l (12,000 gal) of water in their lifetime.

SCURVY!

In the past, sailors on long voyages could not eat fresh vegetables and fruit, so they did not get enough vitamin C. This caused a disease called scurvy. The sailors got sore arms and legs, and their teeth fell out!

Vitamins are chemicals that your body needs to work properly. **Eggs** contain every vitamin except vitamin C.

SUPER STAPLES

The foods you should eat most of are the 'staple' foods, such as pasta, rice or potatoes. They give you a lot of energy.

In the UK, about 165 billion cups of **tea** are drunk each year! The tea bag was first invented in 1908 in New York, United States.

PACKED WITH PROTEIN

Another thing your body needs is protein. The foods that give you the most protein are meat, fish and cheese.

Fish is really good for you. As well as protein, it contains chemicals that help your brain to work! The Japanese eat fish raw, in sushi and sashimi.

JUST ONE!

You do not need a lot of sugar in your diet. You only need a moderate amount of fat as well. Biscuits and cakes should be a treat you only have sometimes.

Fizzy drinks are full of sugar and are not healthy. Water is much better for you!

GROWING IT

All over the world, people are growing food. Some people grow enough food to feed their families, but farmers and food manufacturers grow enough to sell in shops. Growing food to feed the 7 billion people in the world is a big task! Modern technology has helped us to develop ways to grow food on a huge scale.

Soybeans contain lots of protein and are easy to grow, so they are used to make many foods. They are grown in large areas of North and South America.

A HUGE SCALE

Wheat is the world's most widely grown plant. There are huge areas of wheat fields in the United States, and a lot of the wheat grown is used to make bread and pasta. Americans eat 35,000 tonnes (38581 tons) of pasta every year!

Up to 80 per cent of the world's food crops are **pollinated** by insects, such as bees. This helps the crops to make new seeds!

Farmers who grow food as a business often use **chemicals** on their crops to keep the pests and weeds away. These chemicals can cause pollution to the soil and nearby streams and lakes, which harms our natural environments.

Some farmers use their land to rear animals instead of growing crops. Modern **cattle farms** can be very big and are home to thousands of cows!

There are more than 40,000 different kinds of **rice** that we eat. Most of the world's rice is grown in Asia.

Slash and burn is a wasteful way of growing food. Land is burnt to clear it of plants, then it is used to grow crops. When the soil is no longer fertile, the farmers move on and find new land to clear. Huge areas of the Amazon rainforest in South America have been destroyed in this way.

TRADITIONAL WAYS

In poorer countries, many people grow food in traditional ways, without large and complicated machinery. In Ethiopia, Africa, these farmers are winnowing their crop, to separate the seeds from the stalks.

Many people living in **cities** want to grow their own food. All you need is a bit of space and a few boxes of soil. It won't feed the world, but it will taste great!

Organic farming does not use chemicals on crops. Farmers use seaweed or manure (animal poo!) to grow their crops instead, which costs more money but is better for the environment.

FEEDING THE WORLD

With modern technology, it should be possible to grow enough food to feed all the people in the world. Sadly, the food that we grow doesn't reach some poorer countries. In rich parts of the world, people have access to plenty of food and many people eat too much! In poor parts of the world, many people do not have enough to eat because they can't afford to grow or buy food.

FOOD AND DRINKS

① More people in the world are suffering from obesity than from hunger. Obesity means being obese, or very overweight. It comes from eating too much food, especially the wrong kinds of food.

② Coffee is the most popular hot drink in the world. More than 400 billion cups are drunk worldwide each year! Coffee beans are grown commercially in more than 45 countries, but one-third of the world's coffee comes from Brazil.

A HUGE EFFORT

Honeybee workers must visit 2 million flowers to make a 500 g (1 pound) jar of honey. That's a lot of flowers!

GROWING IT YOURSELF

You only need a small piece of land to grow food. It is fun to plant a few seeds and watch the plants grow, then harvest your own food to cook and eat.

FRIGHTENED IN THE KITCHEN?

The fear of cooking is known as Mageirocophobia. Some people are afraid of the cooking process, while others are afraid of cooking for others.

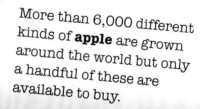

Rice is the staple food for half of the world's population, mostly in Asia. In India, rice is associated with good fortune and the Hindu goddess of wealth, Lakshmi.

FOOD ON THE MOVE

Recipes from some countries have spread around the world after people have visited those places and enjoyed the food. Chinese and Indian food, for example, are now popular all around the world.

More than 6,000 different kinds of **apple** are grown around the world but only a handful of these are available to buy.

GETTING IT HERE

We eat food from all over the world and it sometimes has to travel very far to reach us. Food transportation is big business! These lemons are on their way from California, in the United States, to the rest of the world.

FANTASTIC FRUITS

They are juicy, they are sweet – everyone loves to eat fruit! Fruit is good for us and it is an important part of a healthy diet. There are thousands of different fruits grown and eaten around the world. Some are more unusual than others.

The **pineapple** plant has more than 200 flowers on it, which join together to create one pineapple fruit.

RECORD BREAKER

As of 2013, the world record for the heaviest watermelon is for one grown by Chris Kent in Tennessee, United States. The watermelon weighed in at a whopping 159 kg (350.5 lb)!

Tomatoes have seeds on the inside so they are actually a fruit, not a vegetable. Pumpkins and cucumbers are fruits, too, for the same reason.

Peaches were once known as Persian apples. In China, they are symbols of long life and good luck.

In 2008, the people of Pingyuan County in China created a huge **fruit mosaic**. The mosaic was made using 372,525 fruits and celebrated the work of the region's fruit growers.

Christopher Columbus took orange seeds to America in 1493 and there are now more than 600 varieties of orange worldwide! There are usually ten segments inside an orange.

SOWING SEEDS

The fruit of a plant is the part that stores and then spreads its seeds, so that the plant can reproduce.

The **durian fruit** that grows in Asia really stinks! The smell is so bad that it is even banned from many public places. Despite its stinky scent, it's delicious to eat!

APPLES EVERYWHERE

Apple trees first grew in Central Asia, before they spread across the world. European explorers took them to the Americas. Today, in the United States, 36 states grow apples.

Strawberries are not really fruits because their seeds are on the outside. Technically, a fruit contains the plant's seeds on the inside.

VEGETABLE MARVELS

There are thousands of different kinds of vegetable. Today, we can grow, buy and eat vegetables from all over the world. Wherever they come from, we need to eat a lot of them to stay healthy.

POISONOUS POTATOES

Potato plants are related to a poisonous plant known as deadly nightshade. Both can contain a poison called solanine. Green bits on a potato skin may contain solanine, so be sure to remove them!

The fear of vegetables is called **lachanophobia**.

Carrots were originally purple. In the seventeenth century, growers in the Netherlands developed an orange variety for the Dutch royal family, which was called the House of Orange.

Peppers (or bell peppers) can be red, green, yellow or orange. Red peppers are ripened green ones, so they are the sweetest.

The longest **carrot** ever grown was 5.841 m (19 ft 1.96 in) long! That's huge! It was grown in the UK in 2007.

The most hated vegetable is the **Brussels sprout!** Brussels sprouts are like miniature cabbages with a slightly bitter taste – but they a good for you!

SPECIAL ONIONS

The ancient Romans called onions 'large pearls'. They were a highly prized vegetable. The ancient Egyptians really loved them, too. They buried them with their kings, or pharaohs, and presented baskets full of them as funeral offerings.

Beetroot contains a strong red dye. In the past, it was used to dye cloth to make clothes. Eating a lot of beetroot turns your urine pink!

EAT A RAINBOW

You should try to eat a range of vegetables every day, because they all contain different vitamins that your body needs. Choose those that are the brightest and eat as many shades as possible.

BRILLIANT BEANS

Baked beans are delicious and they are healthy, too. They contain a lot of protein and not much fat.

EATING MEAT

Most people around the world eat meat as part of their diet. In poorer countries, people often eat less meat than people in richer countries. Some people choose not to eat meat at all; they are vegetarians. Vegans choose not to eat any animal products at all!

People in India eat the least meat of anywhere in the world. This is partly because the main religion there is **Hinduism** and Hindus do not eat meat.

A SMALL MOUTHFUL

Insects contain the highest levels of protein and the lowest amounts of fat. These are fried grasshoppers!

A MEATY DIET

The most eaten meat by weight in the world is pork, but the meat eaten by the most people in the world is goat.

More than 50 billion **chickens** are reared every year for their meat. Some of them are reared outdoors, while others live indoors, in sheds.

Meat is expensive to produce because animals take up a lot of land and eat a lot of grain. It takes nearly 6 kg (13 lb) of grain to produce around 450 g (1 lb) of beef.

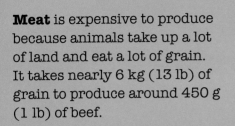

AN EARLY START

Goats were the first animals to be kept for their meat, probably about 10,000 years ago.

Some animal farmers are **nomadic**. This means that they travel around with their herds, looking for fresh grazing land. These nomads are in Mongolia, Asia.

The meat of the **bison** has less fat than beef. You can get a lot of meat from one animal!

Did you know?

In 2009, a survey found that about 3 per cent of the UK's population is **vegetarian**.

DELICIOUS DAIRY

Foods made from milk are dairy products. Butter, cheese and ice cream are all dairy products. They contain calcium, which makes our bones strong. They also contain a lot of fat, so we shouldn't eat too much of them. There are thousands of different cheeses made around the world. It would take a lifetime to try them all!

DAIRY FANS

The most dairy products are eaten in countries where dairy cattle are reared. In countries where they do not rear animals for milk, people eat far fewer dairy products. Their bodies may even not be able to digest them properly, and they may have a bad reaction if they eat them.

WHICH ANIMALS?

The most common animals that are reared for their milk are cows, but sheep and goats are also farmed for milk.

Gorgonzola is a kind of Italian cheese. It has veins of blue fungus in it. It has been made in northern Italy since the year CE 879!

MILKING BUFFALO?

The milk from buffalo is used to make a cheese called mozzarella, which you will often find on your pizza! It is also used to make ice cream.

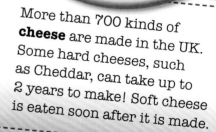

More than 700 kinds of **cheese** are made in the UK. Some hard cheeses, such as Cheddar, can take up to 2 years to make! Soft cheese is eaten soon after it is made.

In 1856, French scientist **Louis Pasteur** discovered that heating milk to a high temperature kills the bacteria in it. This process is called pasteurization, and it protects the purity and taste of the milk we buy.

A PINT OF CAMEL?

In desert countries in the Middle East, people drink the milk of camels. It has more goodness than cow's milk and in those countries it is also used to treat some illnesses.

THE OLDEST CHEESE

In 2014, the oldest-known cheese in the world was found buried in the sand with a mummified body, in the Taklamakan Desert in China. It had been there for 3,600 years! The dry conditions preserved the cheese surprisingly well.

The average person in the United States consumes 26 L (45.8 pints) of ice cream a year.

WHO EATS THAT?

Different people have different ideas of what tastes nice. In some parts of the world, people eat foods that others might think are a bit strange or taste weird! Over the centuries, people have learned to make food from the ingredients available to them.

In Thailand, southeast Asia, people enjoy giant **water bugs** served with chilli and sticky rice. They also like to add dung beetles to their curries.

STINKY TOFU

The name says it all in this fermented tofu dish, which is a popular street food in China. The stench of stinky tofu is decidedly rotten, but when it is well prepared, the taste is surprisingly gentle.

CHEESEY

Many cheeses can smell a bit, but one of the very smelliest is Limburger. It is made in Germany, using the same bacteria that make the human body smell. This is why it reminds you of stinky feet. Gross!

In Ghana, West Africa, **frogs** are on the menu. People like them either roasted or served in a soup!

In Cambodia, people eat fried **tarantula spiders** as a tasty snack. It is a good way of getting rid of them, at least.

In some African countries, the locals eat the fat **mopane worm**. The worms are either cooked in sauce or dried to be crunchy like potato crisps.

In Korea, people eat **octopuses** while they are still alive!

In France, there is a tradition of eating **exotic meats** on Christmas Day. People eat kangaroo, crocodile and ostrich. Once they are cooked, ostrich and kangaroo look like beef.

ROTTING FISH

The Swedish delicacy, surströmming, is fermented fish. This tinned food smells so awful that the official advice is to open the tin outdoors, but then to eat it indoors because the rotten smell attracts flies.

KEEPING IT SAFE

Honey is the only food that can last forever. In time, food begins to go bad and germs grow on it. If we eat these germs, they can make us ill. It is important to know how to stop that from happening. In the past, when there were no fridges or freezers, people thought up clever ways to store fresh ingredients so that they would last longer!

FREEZE!

Foods that we want to eat in more than a few days can be kept in a freezer, where no germs can grow on them! Frozen foods usually have to be defrosted before they are cooked. This means letting them warm to room temperature all the way through.

Keep the food that you are going to eat soon in the **fridge**. The temperature inside must be 5 °C (41 F) or below, to stop germs growing.

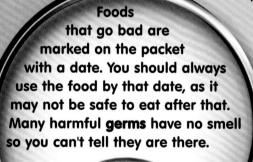

Foods that go bad are marked on the packet with a date. You should always use the food by that date, as it may not be safe to eat after that. Many harmful **germs** have no smell so you can't tell they are there.

12/2014

FOOD POISONING

① Cooking foods at a high temperature kills most of the germs on them. Foods that are not cooked, such as salads and fruit, need to be kept away from foods such as meat, which might have germs on them.

② There are around 1 million cases of food poisoning every year in the UK. There are more cases in summer, because foods go bad faster in warmer weather.

MADE TO LAST

The food with the longest life is honey. Honey from ancient Egypt has been found and is still perfectly good to eat!

Did you know that the **kitchen sink** is likely to contain 100,000 times more germs than the toilet or bathroom? The germs can easily get from the sink into your food.

TAKE CARE WITH CHICKEN

More than half of the raw chicken we buy contains a bacteria called campylobacter, which causes food poisoning. Cooking chicken properly stops you from getting poorly!

In the fridge, **eggs** can absorb smells and other substances from other foods through their shells, so store them in their box.

Every year, almost half of all the food that we produce is wasted. Sometimes, we buy too much food and can't eat it before it goes off.

One way to keep meat and fish safe to eat for a long time is to '**cure**' it. Curing can be done by hanging the meat or fish over a smoky fire, or by soaking it in very salty water.

BRILLIANT BODIES

07

Your body is the most amazing machine ever made! It is so complicated that we still do not know everything about how it works. However, we do know a lot and we are finding out more all the time. The billions of parts of your body work together so you can breathe, move, laugh, eat, sleep, grow and read this book!

HEROIC HUMANS

Humans can't run faster than the speediest animals and we are not the strongest. We cannot fly, or breathe underwater. So why are we so brilliant? Mostly, it is our brains that make us so advanced. Using our brains, we have learned how to feed ourselves, build societies and use the world around us to make our lives better.

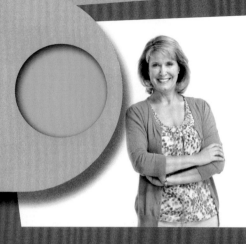

Every atom in your body is billions of years old. **Hydrogen**, the most common element in the universe and a major feature of your body, was produced in the Big Bang 13.7 billion years ago!

HOW MANY?

The average adult weighing 70 kg (154 lb) is made up of around 7 octillion atoms. That's a massive number! Every year, 98 per cent of the atoms are replaced.

We are mammals but instead of our bodies being covered in fur, we have **hair**. The hair on the face grows the fastest.

GROWTH SPURTS!

Humans grow fastest between the ages of 0 and 2. Then, as children, they grow at a steady rate. At about 12–13, a growth spurt starts that lasts for a few years. Girls stop growing at about 16 and boys at about 18 years of age.

The brain and nerve cells are the only **cells** in the body that cannot regenerate. Once brain cells are damaged, they are not replaced.

We are so curious that we want to **explore** space. We have learned how to land on the moon, and we now know a lot about our solar system.

I CAN DO IT!

Humans have achieved fantastic things and are always looking for new ways to be the best. Why else would there be competitions for pulling cars or balancing spoons on your face?

GETTING OLDER

We cannot avoid getting older. We may slow down, but there are some good things about it, too. We catch fewer colds and other bugs, because our bodies have had a long time to become resistant to them. We also hopefully have more wisdom from having lived longer!

On average, women live 6-8 years longer than men.

BRAIN POWER

Your brain controls your body. It does all your thinking and remembering. It also sends out instructions to different parts of your body so you can move, speak and feel. It is connected to the rest of your body by a network of nerves. These nerves carry messages between your brain and the rest of your body.

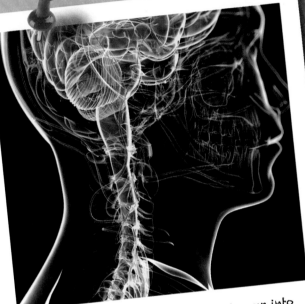

The main bundle of nerves running up into your brain is your **spinal cord**. Smaller nerves branch off it to the rest of your body.

GREY AND WRINKLY

Your brilliant brain is a grey, wrinkled lump weighing about 1.5 kg (3 lb). It has two halves that are joined in the middle. Each part of your brain has its own job to do. The seeing and balance parts are at the back. The thinking and feeling parts are at the front.

Your brain needs a lot of fuel. It uses 20 per cent of all the **oxygen and blood** in your body.

In a lifetime, your **long-term memory** can hold up to 1 quadrillion separate bits of information!

There are so many **nerve cells** in your brain, you would have to count non-stop for more than 3,000 years to count them all!

The **brain** continues developing until you are almost 50 years old.

TIME FOR BED

A person will die from total lack of sleep sooner than from lack of food. You cannot survive more than about 10 days without sleep, but you can last a few weeks without food if you have water.

Only about 10 per cent of people are **left-handed**. Those who can use both hands equally well are called 'ambidextrous'.

Messages travel along your **nerves** at up to 400 kph (250 mph).

SENSATIONAL

We need our senses to tell us all about the world around us. Our five senses are sight, hearing, touch, taste and smell. Through our sense organs, we take in information that is sent to the brain as signals. The brain works out what the signals mean and tells our body how to act.

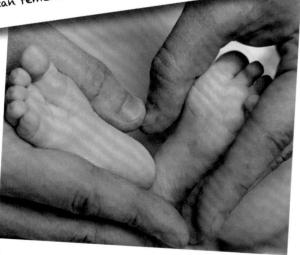

Your sense of **smell** is around 10,000 times more sensitive than your sense of taste. It can remember 50,000 different scents.

BIG EARS

Our ears and noses never stop growing, which is why they often look bigger on old people.

TINY BONE

Sounds are actually very fast movements in the air. Your ears gather sounds from outside and the bones inside your ear make them louder. The smallest bone in your body is inside your ear. The stirrup bone is only 2.8 mm (0.1 in) long.

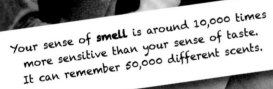

The organ we use for touching is our **skin**. It has millions of nerve endings that tell the brain what something feels like.

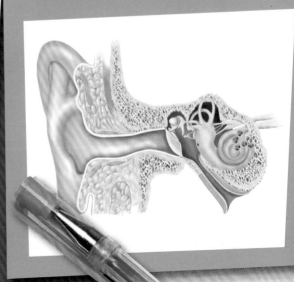

You **taste** using your tongue, which is covered in 3,000–10,000 taste buds.

In Tibet, China, sticking your **tongue** out at someone is a way of greeting them!

Your **eyes** can tell the difference between about 10 million different shades of colours.

EYELASH VISITORS

We all have tiny mites living in our eyelashes, but they are too small to see.

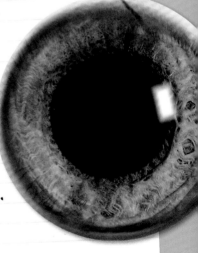

TASTING TONGUE

There are just five different kinds of taste. They are salty, sweet, sour, bitter and savoury.

The black area in the middle of your eye is a hole called the **pupil**. It widens in the dark, to let more light into your eye, but gets smaller in bright light.

A PERFECT SYSTEM

Blood is the transport system that takes oxygen and food to everywhere it needs to go. It also carries waste materials away, so that your body can get rid of them. Your heart is the brilliant muscle that keeps this system moving all the time!

Blood travels around your body through **blood vessels**. The main ones branch off into a network that becomes smaller and smaller. Altogether, they are about 96,500 km (60,000 miles) long, which is twice the distance around the Earth!

LUNG POWER

Your right lung is slightly bigger than your left and takes in more air. Two-thirds of the heart is found on the left side of the body.

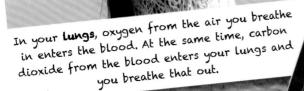

In your **lungs**, oxygen from the air you breathe in enters the blood. At the same time, carbon dioxide from the blood enters your lungs and you breathe that out.

If you opened your **lungs** and spread them out, they would cover an area the size of a tennis court!

You cannot stop **breathing**. You can hold your breath for a minute or two, but even if that makes you faint, you will automatically start to breathe again.

When you **exercise**, you breathe more quickly to get more air into your lungs. Your heart pumps faster, too, to get the oxygen to your muscles.

BREATHE EASILY

Some people have an illness called asthma. It makes the muscles in the tubes entering the lungs tight, so less air can get in. A puff of a special medicine from an inhaler makes the muscle relax again, so sufferers can breathe more easily.

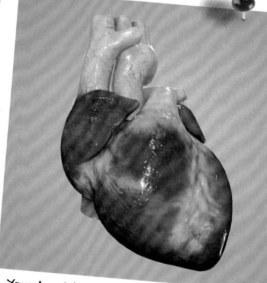

Your **heart** beats around 100,000 times a day, and 36,500,000 times a year. By the time you are 30, it will have beaten more than 1 billion times!

 If your heart or lungs become **diseased** and stop working properly, it is possible to have either (or both) of them replaced.

KEEPING MOVING

Our skeleton of bones is what gives us our shape. Adults have 206 bones in their bodies, some big ones and some tiny ones. They have more than 600 muscles attached to them. Together, the muscles and bones work to move us around so we can sit, stand, run and jump.

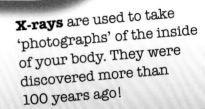

X-rays are used to take 'photographs' of the inside of your body. They were discovered more than 100 years ago!

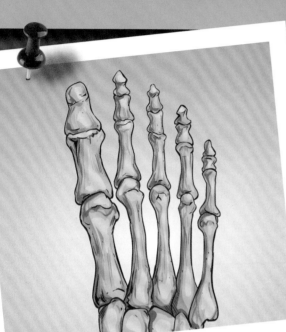

Your **foot** has 26 bones in it. Some of your toe bones are very small. A quarter of the bones in the human body are found in the feet!

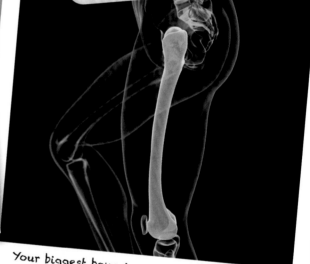

Your biggest bone is your thigh bone, called the **femur**. It is connected to your hip at the top and your knee at the bottom. The femur is stronger than concrete!

The bones and muscles in your **legs** work together in a complex way to help you walk. So far, scientists have been unable to make a robot that has the same structure.

BIG BITE

The strongest muscle in your body is your jaw muscle. Like all muscles, it is made of bundles of fibres.

It is amazing that **bones** are strong because they are 31 per cent water!

SLEEP TO GROW

We are about 1 cm (0.4 in) taller in the morning than in the evening. This is because during the day, the bits between our bones are squashed by activities such as standing and sitting.

Your most active muscles are in your eyes. They move about **100,000** times a day.

FLEXIBLE JOINTS

The places where your bones meet are called joints. Some joints, such as elbows and knees, can move only in one direction. Others, such as hips, can move round and round.

Your bones also protect the soft parts of your body inside. Your **skull** is the bone that protects your brain. Your ribs protect your heart and lungs.

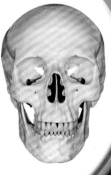

EAT TO GROW

Your body's fuel is air and food. Food gives you energy to keep busy through the day and to grow. Your body is brilliant at breaking down the food you eat, to get all the useful materials, called nutrients, out of it. This process is called digestion. It starts as soon as you take a bite.

Your mouth makes a liquid called **saliva**, or spit, to start the process of breaking down food. The average person produces enough saliva in a lifetime to fill two swimming pools!

HOW LONG?

It can take more than a day for the food you eat to travel all the way through your body.

Your **teeth** are coated with a layer of enamel. This is the hardest substance in your body. It can be worn away by sugar and other foods if you do not clean your teeth properly.

There are more **bacteria** living in your mouth than there are people in the world! They rarely do you any harm, though.

Your first teeth are called 'milk teeth'. They start growing 6–7 months before you are born.

Your body replaces the lining of your **stomach** every 3-4 days, so that the strong acids do not digest your stomach.

OUCH!

The real work on your food begins in your stomach. It contains strong liquids called acids. If your stomach acid got on your skin, it would burn a hole in it!

Your **liver** is a big organ with nearly 500 jobs to do. One of those jobs is taking the good stuff from food out of your blood, then sending it on for other parts of the body to use.

TUMMY RUMBLES

When your tummy rumbles, it is the sound of the muscles in the walls of your stomach and intestines moving in and out. The noise is louder when your stomach is empty.

INTERESTING INTESTINES

Food leaves the stomach and enters the small and large intestine. The good bits pass through the walls of the intestines and into your blood. The bits you don't need leave your body as poo!

159

WRAP IT UP

Skin is the biggest organ in your body. It is full of nerve endings which send messages to your brain about pressure, pain, heat and cold. It also protects you against harm from germs, the sun and the cold. Hairs in your skin add an extra layer of protection.

The thickest skin on your body is on the **palms of your hands** and the soles of your feet. The thinnest is on your eyelids.

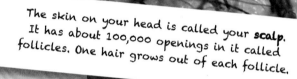

The skin on your head is called your **scalp**. It has about 100,000 openings in it called follicles. One hair grows out of each follicle.

DUST OR WHAT?

The dust in your home is mostly made of dead skin cells from you and your family. The top layer of your skin flakes off once every 4 weeks!

STOP TICKLING!

The nerve endings in your skin respond to touch. You have nerve endings in your fingers, too, so your brain responds to tickling in a different way.

When you get cold, tiny muscles under your skin pull the base of the hairs, making them stand upright. This traps warm air close to your skin. The muscles also make the little lumps in your skin called **goosebumps**.

DEAD HAIR

Hair is mostly made of dead cells packed with a substance called keratin. The only living part of hair is at its root, under your skin.

Your skin is full of tiny holes, called **pores**. When your body gets too warm, a salty liquid called sweat oozes out of them. It takes heat away from your skin, to cool you down.

Skin can be pale pink to dark brown. It all depends on how much pigment you have in your skin. The **pigment** is called melanin. Pale skin lets more sunlight into the skin than dark skin, so the skin burns more easily.

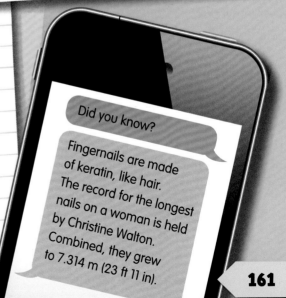

Did you know?

Fingernails are made of keratin, like hair. The record for the longest nails on a woman is held by Christine Walton. Combined, they grew to 7.314 m (23 ft 11 in).

REPAIR AND RENEW

Everybody feels ill sometimes. It's not fun, but usually we get better quite quickly! Your body is brilliant at repairing itself. When it comes under attack from germs and other diseases, it goes into battle mode. All systems work together to defeat the enemy and make you better.

In **old age**, new body cells are less powerful. This means that you have less strength and your eyesight and hearing weakens with age.

OUCH!

When you have cut yourself and it is bleeding, your skin and blood start to work together. Blood cells stick together to make a patch over the wound and the skin forms a scab.

GETTING OLDER

After the age of about 25–35, the body is less able to renew itself perfectly. The new cells are a little less effective than the ones they replace. At this age, you are still healthy and active, though.

CLEVER YOU

Every minute, a healthy young body makes about 300 million new cells, to replace the ones that naturally wear out and die.

Germs can get into your body through a cut or through your mouth. Once inside, the germs can multiply very quickly.

You can protect yourself from getting ill in lots of ways. Keep clean, to wash away germs. Do lots of **exercise**, to keep your heart and lungs in good shape. Eat well, to give your body what it needs.

ALLERGIC

The system in your body that protects you from disease is called your immune system. Allergies happen when your immune system decides to attack a substance that is harmless. Some people are allergic to nuts, for example. Others are allergic to dairy products. An allergy to the pollen in plants is called hayfever.

SLEEP TIGHT

Having a good night's sleep is the best way to let your body renew itself. In the morning, you will wake up refreshed and ready for anything!

LIFE STORIES

Ask anyone who has lived a long life and they will tell you that the secret is to keep active. Many of the world's oldest people were still taking regular exercise in their 80s and 90s, even their 100s! They also say that they eat properly and sleep well. Some people have lived long lives and others have broken records in weird and wonderful ways, using their unique body parts!

Former South African President **Nelson Mandela** lived to be 95 years old. The average life expectancy in South Africa is about 53 years.

THREE CENTURIES

It is more than 15 years since the new century began in 2000, but some people have seen three centuries in their lifetime. One of them was a Japanese woman who was born in 1898. At 117 years of age, she was the oldest living person, until her death in 2015.

THAT'S OLD

The record for the oldest person who ever lived was a French woman called Jeanne Calment. When she died in 1997, she was 122 years and 164 days old. She was still riding a bicycle at the age of 100.

In 2005, an Australian man named *Smoky Dawson* released an album of new songs he had written. He was 92 years old!

The longest **beard** on a living person measured 2.37 metres (7 ft 9 in) in 2010. It belonged to Sarwan Singh of Canada.

The tallest man ever was **Robert Wadlow** from the United States. In 1940, he measured 2.72 m (8 ft 11.1 in) tall. He had the biggest feet ever, too. They were 47 cm (18.5 in) long.

The longest fingernails ever measured belonged to Lee Redmond of the United States. They grew to 8.65 m (28 ft 4.6 in) in 2008.

100 YEARS

ROYAL CONGRATULATIONS

In the UK, when you reach your 100th birthday, you may receive a message of congratulations from the Queen. More than 13,000 people are over 100 years old in the UK today.

In the UK, in 2014, a woman could expect to **live** to 82.6 years old and a man to 78.7 years. Many more people now live to be 90 years old than they did 10 years ago.

DEADLY DISEASES

There are thousands of different diseases that can make us sick. Some are infectious, so we can catch them from other people. Others might be inherited from our parents. Some, we catch from organisms in the environment. Luckily, doctors now understand a lot about many diseases and they can treat people back to good health.

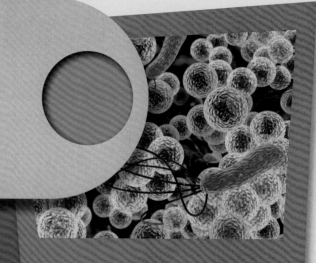

Infectious diseases can be caught from someone else if you come into contact with them. Chickenpox and colds are infectious.

VIRAL OR BACTERIAL

Infectious diseases are mostly caused by two kinds of tiny organisms called viruses and bacteria. They are spread through the air, on animals or in water.

Tuberculosis (TB) is an infectious disease caused by bacteria that affects the lungs. Each year, about 9 million people around the world suffer from the disease, and more than 1 million people die from it.

SMALL BUT DEADLY

① Viruses are very small, but they can be deadly. Inside the body, they invade living cells and force them to make a lot of copies of the virus. These then spread out through the body. Viruses cause some serious diseases, such as measles. They also cause the flu.

② Viruses are usually around 100 times smaller than bacteria. The ebola virus is particularly dangerous. It causes a very bad fever and about half of people who catch it, die. It occurs mainly in Africa.

When one infectious disease affects many people at once across a large area, it is called an **epidemic**. Epidemics of flu happen every few years, usually in winter.

PANDEMIC!

When an epidemic of a disease spreads to more than one continent, and affects millions of people, it is called a pandemic. There were several flu pandemics around the world in the twentieth century.

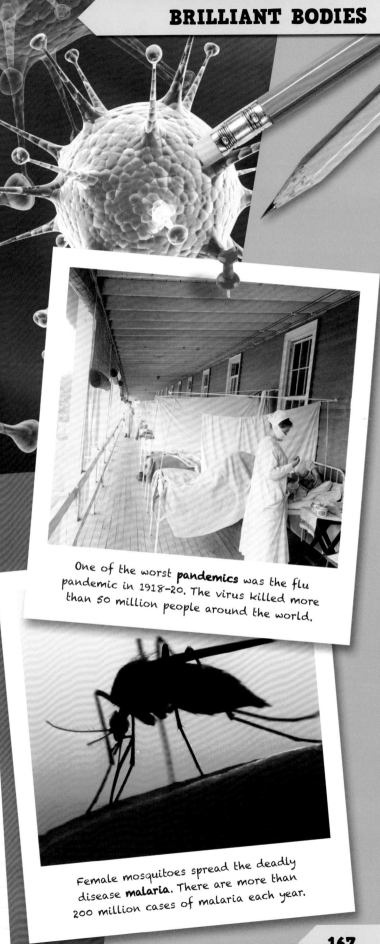

One of the worst **pandemics** was the flu pandemic in 1918–20. The virus killed more than 50 million people around the world.

Some diseases are not infectious. **Cancer** is a disease where some cells grow too quickly and form a lump. Scientists are working to develop treatments for these kinds of diseases.

Female mosquitoes spread the deadly disease **malaria**. There are more than 200 million cases of malaria each year.

167

MEDICAL MARVELS

Our understanding of medicine is improving all the time. Scientists and doctors are working hard to find better ways to diagnose diseases, which means working out which disease a person has. Once they know that, they can work on the best ways to treat it. The best thing is to prevent diseases happening in the first place. Medicine is developing all the time to help aid prevention and improve survival rates.

Until the late 1800s, people did not even know that germs, called **bacteria**, were the cause of many diseases. A French scientist named Louis Pasteur worked it out and proved it.

VALUABLE VACCINES

Vaccines protect people from getting a disease. The vaccine gives the person a tiny, harmless bit of the disease. The body can then work out how to fight that disease if it comes into contact with it.

DRUGS DO IT

Fewer than 100 years ago, scientists discovered antibiotics. These drugs can kill the bacteria that cause diseases. Antibiotics have transformed medicine and saved millions of lives.

Doctors know that some people are more likely to get certain diseases, such as **cancer**, so they test everyone who is at risk.

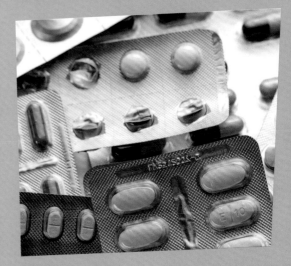

Antibiotics cannot kill viruses. New drugs are being developed to stop viruses multiplying inside the body. You have to take these drugs early on in the illness for them to work.

75 mg

Tamiflu® 75

Hartkapseln

Oseltamivir

10 Kapseln

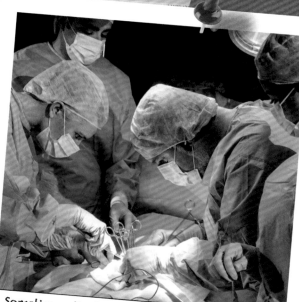

Sometimes, the best way to treat an illness is through **surgery**. This means opening up the body and repairing or removing the damaged part.

WORLD HEALTH

The World Health Organization (WHO) has the job of looking at international public health. It can create health campaigns and respond when outbreaks happen. World Health Day is on 7th April each year.

BEATING CANCER

Doctors are now much better at treating cancer than in the past. Scientists understand more about how cancers develop and are making new drugs to attack them. Millions of pounds are spent on cancer research every year.

It's simple. **Soap** kills bacteria. Just washing your hands with soap several times a day is a great way to protect your body from diseases.

NEW FRONTIERS

Thousands of people around the world are working to make medicine even better. Some of them are scientists working in laboratories. Others are doctors and surgeons, who are learning from their patients. Some are nurses and other carers, who are looking after the sick. The future for world medicine is certainly bright.

New **technology** has developed simple tests that can determine which illness a person has. More than 100 million of these tests are now in use worldwide.

DRUG DISCOVERY

Scientists have made many drugs that can cure people of diseases they would have died from in the past. They are always looking for ways to improve old drugs and invent new ones.

A new type of **vaccine** is being developed. A patch containing the vaccine is stuck onto the skin for a few minutes. This makes it cheaper and easier to vaccinate people in rural areas.

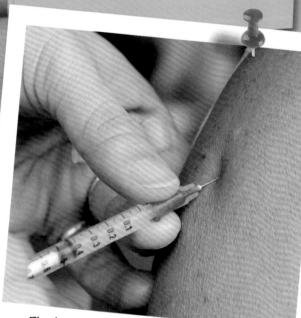

The biggest killers are diseases, such as **malaria**, which hit millions of people in poor countries. Scientists are working hard to develop a malaria vaccine.

CLUES IN THE GENES

Our genes are the instructions in our cells that make us what we are. They decide everything about us, including any diseases we may have inherited. Scientists know a lot about the codes in our genes and use that knowledge to find ways to treat diseases.

Scientists have found that some viruses kill **bacteria**. They are working on ways to use these viruses to kill bacteria in the body that are causing disease.

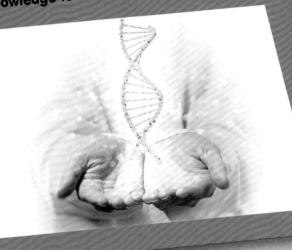

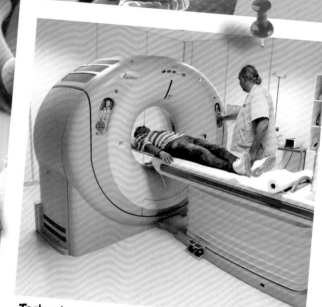

Another important step in the fight against diseases is cracking the **genetic code** of the viruses and bacteria that cause them. This will help scientists to develop more effective drugs.

Technology has brought us incredible new ways to see inside the human body. Scanners can take very clear pictures of what is going on, so doctors can decide how to treat the patient.

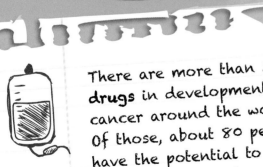

There are more than 3,000 **drugs** in development for cancer around the world. Of those, about 80 per cent have the potential to be all-new treatments.

SCIENCE SOLUTIONS

Science is the study of the world around us, what it is made of and how it works. Over the centuries, scientists have learned a huge amount about the world, but there is still a lot more to find out.

WHAT'S THE MATTER?

Everything we can see, touch, smell or taste is made of matter. Matter is made up of particles. They are so small that we can see them only through a powerful microscope. Not everything is matter, though. Light, sound and heat are not matter. They are forms of energy. So everything that exists is either matter or energy.

Matter is made of atoms, which are tiny particles. There are about 100 different kinds of atom. Our bodies are made of 28 kinds. Water is made of two kinds: hydrogen (H) and oxygen (O).

WHAT STATE?

Matter comes in three different forms or states. These are solid, liquid and gas. In a solid, the atoms are held together in a definite shape. Some solids are soft and stretchy, others are hard and strong. Copper is hard but it can be stretched into long pipes or wires.

WANDERING GASES

Gases flow to fill any container they are put into, but they will not stay still. They have no fixed shape because there is a lot of space between each of their particles. The gas carbon dioxide can be held in a liquid to make it fizzy. You can see the bubbles of gas.

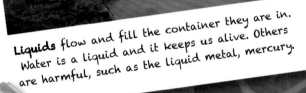

Liquids flow and fill the container they are in. Water is a liquid and it keeps us alive. Others are harmful, such as the liquid metal, mercury.

When it gets hotter or colder, **matter** can change from one **state** to another. Water is a solid when it is ice, it is a liquid when it is water and it is a gas when it is steam.

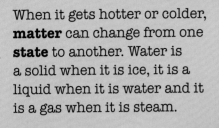

Solid **metals** have to be made very, very hot before they turn into liquids. They can then be poured into casts to make useful things. They become solid again when they cool down.

NO RETURN

Some kinds of matter can be turned from a liquid to a solid and back again. Others are irreversible. When you heat a liquid egg, for example, it becomes a solid. When it cools down, it does not turn back into a liquid!

PUTTING ATOMS TOGETHER

Different kinds of atom can be put together to make new materials. Salt is made of two kinds of atom, called sodium and chlorine. Over 90 per cent of the human body is made from hydrogen, oxygen and carbon.

In 1778, French scientist **Antoine Lavoisier** was the first person to discover and name oxygen gas. In 1783, he discovered hydrogen gas.

175

POWER TO THE WORLD

Everything you do needs energy. All animals get their energy from food and plants get theirs from the sun. The things we have made in our world, such as ships and cars, need energy, too. We get this energy from several different sources.

Light and heat are the main kinds of **energy** on Earth, and they both come from the sun. Without this energy, we would not exist.

STORED ENERGY

Energy from the sun is stored in the strangest places. Coal, oil and gas deep underground are the remains of plants and animals that lived millions of years ago, and have been squashed down. Those animals and plants contain old energy from the sun.

We take **oil** out of the ground and use it to make fuels. These fuels provide the energy to drive cars, trucks and planes.

We release the energy stored in our **food** when we eat and digest it. The amount of energy foods we contain is measured in kilocalories, or calories (kcal) for short.

120 kcal

300 kcal

80 kcal

The energy from 1 l (0.3 gal) of **fuel** will drive a car about 16 km (10 miles). If you used the same amount of energy to pedal a bicycle, you could travel over 500 km (310 miles).

In the past, before engines were invented, the only way to power ships was with the wind. **Ships** had huge sails to catch the energy of the wind. If the wind did not blow, sailors were stuck until it started again.

HEAT ENERGY

We use heat energy to cook our food outdoors. Some people also like to light a fire in their homes, for its heat and its beauty.

Before **electricity** was invented, candles, gas lamps or oil lamps were used to light homes and streets. These light sources were smelly, and did not give off a lot of light.

Every second, the amount of **energy** that reaches Earth from the sun is equal to that which a coal-fired power station could make from about 200,000 truckloads of coal!

AWESOME ELECTRICITY

Electricity powers so much of what we do. Without it in our homes, there would be no computers, lights, television, fridge or washing machine. A lot of the electricity we make comes from burning coal, oil or gas, in huge power stations.

Electricity speeds through the wires in our houses at more than 1,600 kph (994 mph).

RAW POWER

The best way to see the power of electricity is in lightning. Lightning bolts can reach nearly 30,000 °C (54,032 F). That is almost six times hotter than the surface of the sun!

It would take 25,000 fireflies to give out the same light as one household light bulb.

CRAZY HAIR

When you rub a balloon against your head, you create an electrical charge on your hairs, which makes them stand up.

The burning of **coal** is used to produce more than 40 per cent of the world's electricity.

The first reliable electric **light bulb** was invented by Thomas Edison in the 1870s. It was not nearly as bright as light bulbs are today.

BRILLIANT!

The American Thomas Edison was a brilliant scientist. He invented more than 2,000 electrical things, including light switches and plug sockets.

POWER TO THE PEOPLE

① A huge network of cables carries electricity from power stations across the country to where it is needed.

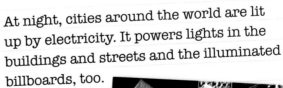

② At night, cities around the world are lit up by electricity. It powers lights in the buildings and streets and the illuminated billboards, too.

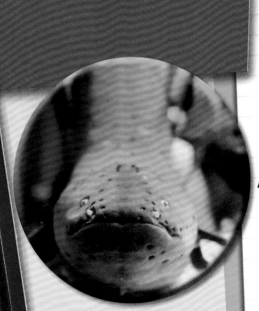

Electric **eels** can produce electric shocks strong enough to stun a person.

AN ENDLESS SUPPLY

We do not have an unlimited supply of coal, oil and gas in the ground. One day, they will all run out. We must find new ways to make enough electricity to power our growing world. Research is being done on ways to use different resources, such as renewable energy. These are powered by water, wind and sunshine.

The wind will still be blowing long after all the coal and oil have run out. **Wind turbines** have blades that turn in the wind, making electricity.

SHINE ON

Panels made of special materials like silicon can convert sunlight into electricity. Each house with solar panels stores its own electricity to use when it is needed.

Flowing **water** contains a lot of energy. Some electricity is made using the force of moving water in the tides in coastal areas.

Water power is collected by building a **dam** across a powerful river. The Three Gorges Dam in China is the largest dam in the world that is used to produce electricity.

Electricity made from the movement of water is called **hydroelectric power**. The first ever hydroelectric power station was built at Niagara Falls, in the United States, in 1895. It was designed by the scientist Nikola Tesla.

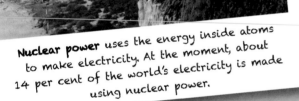

Nuclear power uses the energy inside atoms to make electricity. At the moment, about 14 per cent of the world's electricity is made using nuclear power.

UNDERGROUND HEAT

Geothermal energy plants take their power from the heat in the ground. They work by pumping cold water down a hole drilled into the earth. The water heats up and it returns to the surface as hot water and steam. These are then used to make electricity.

TOXIC WASTE

Nuclear power does not cause pollution but it creates waste material that is dangerous. It is difficult to store it safely because it stays dangerous for many years.

CAUTIO
RADIOACTIV

Did you know?

Scientists have discovered that electricity can even be produced from the energy in human poo!

FEEL THE FORCE

A force is a push or a pull on an object. When you kick a ball, you push it. When a crane lifts a heavy load, it is pulling it up. Forces cause objects to move, or change their speed or direction. Forces can also change an object's shape. Some forces can be seen when one object touches another. Other forces are working all the time, but we cannot see them.

We use our **muscles** to produce a force. The stronger your muscles, the stronger the force you make. A weightlifter pulls the weights up to his chest, then pushes them up into the air.

WORLD RECORD

At the Olympic Games in 2012, North Korea's weightlifter, Un Guk Kim, broke the world record by lifting an incredible 327 kg (721 lb). That is like lifting four adult men above your head at the same time.

Scientist **Isaac Newton** discovered gravity in the 1600s when he watched an apple fall off a tree.

GRAVITY PULLING

When you drop something, it falls to the ground. The force called gravity is what pulls it down. Everything on Earth is held down by gravity. You cannot see gravity, but without it, we would all float away!

Your **weight** on the moon is only about one sixth of your weight on Earth, because there is so much less gravity there.

Friction is a force that stops things moving. When you sit on a grassy slope, friction stops you sliding down it. The surfaces are both rough and rub against each other. When you go skating, there is not much friction between your skates and the ice, so you slide along easily.

GETTING HOTTER

Friction can make things hotter. The brake pads in a car's wheels rub against the wheel, using friction to slow them down. They get very hot in the process.

The shapes of **trains, cars and planes** are specially designed to reduce the amount of friction between them and the air. This is called making them streamlined.

MIGHTY MAGNETS

Another force that is important to us is magnetic force. It attracts some metals, especially iron and steel. A magnet has two ends, or poles, called north and south.

The needle of a **compass** is a magnet. It always points towards Earth's magnetic North Pole.

LIGHT FOR ALL

Light is a form of energy. It can travel freely through the air. When you wake up in the morning, you can see the world around you because it is lit up by the sun, even if it is a cloudy day. At night, when the sun has set, we have to make our own light, using electricity or flames.

SHINING?

Anything that gives off light, such as a torch, is called luminous. Most things are not luminous. They seem bright because they are lit up by something else. The sun is luminous, but the moon is not. It only seems to 'shine' because its surface reflects light from the sun.

Light travels in **waves**. It travels incredibly fast, 1080 million kph (670 million mph). That is the fastest speed of anything in the universe.

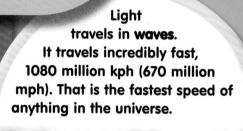

Even the light from the sun can be blocked by the moon, if it passes between Earth and the sun. Although this event is rare, it is spectacular. We call it a solar **eclipse**.

Light travels in straight lines, so it cannot go around objects. When an object blocks light, a dark area forms behind it. This is called a shadow.

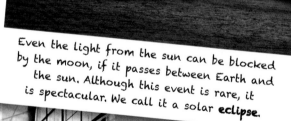

Shadows are not totally black. They have a darkest part, called the umbra, and a slightly lighter part, called the penumbra. A few light rays have reached this area.

TRANSPARENT OR TRANSLUCENT?

Some solids can let light pass through them. They are called **transparent**. Clear glass is transparent, but frosted glass lets some light through. We call it **translucent**.

Solids with a shiny surface make light bounce off them. This is called **reflection**. Mirrors reflect light. If the mirror is flat, your reflection is normal. If it is wavy, you get an odd reflection.

BENDING LIGHT

A beam of light can be bent by passing it through a curved piece of glass, called a lens. A magnifying glass bends light, to make the objects you are looking at seem bigger.

TOO FAR OR TOO SMALL

We can use lenses in lots of different ways. They are in the glasses we wear to improve our vision. They are in the telescopes we use to look at things far away in space. They are also in the microscopes we use to see things that are too small for us to see with our own eyes. These blood cells from the human body can be seen only with a microscope.

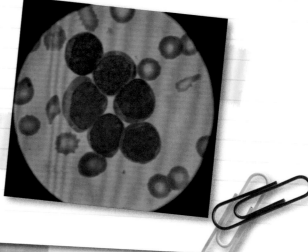

RAINBOW WORLD

Around us are thousands of different colours and shades and our eyes are brilliant at telling them all apart. If you have ever tried to identify objects using only your sense of touch, you will know how tricky that can be. Our eyes confirm what we know. If an object is green and round, it is probably an apple, right?

Objects look a certain colour because they either reflect or absorb those colours. An apple looks green because it absorbs all the colours in light except **green**. The green light is reflected to us, and we see a green apple.

In 1666, **Isaac Newton** first suggested that white light can be separated into different bands.

BLACK AND WHITE

Black objects look black because they have absorbed all the colours in the light spectrum. In contrast, white objects reflect back all the colours in the light spectrum.

HOW DOES IT WORK?

Sunlight looks white or yellow, but it is actually a mixture of light from many different colours. This is called the spectrum of light. You can see the spectrum when white light shines onto a solid pyramid of glass, called a prism. It splits the light into all its bands.

Rainbows happen when droplets of water in the air act like prisms and break white light up into seven colours. They are red, orange, yellow, green, blue, indigo and violet.

If you look at a **rainbow** from up in a plane, it appears as a complete circle round the sun!

A STRIKING DISPLAY

At sunset, light from the sun travels through a thicker layer of Earth's atmosphere than when it is high overhead in the middle of the day. Particles in the atmosphere scatter the blue part of sunlight away from Earth, so the sky seems to turn red.

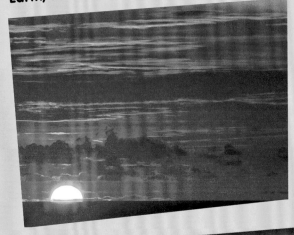

The three **primary colours** of the light spectrum are red, blue and green. They can be combined in thousands of different ways to make other colours. So red and blue make purple, and red and green make yellow.

Did you know?

Some people cannot tell the difference between bluish and greenish colours, and yellowish and reddish colours.

TAKING PICTURES

Cameras are used to take pictures. They can be still pictures, like photos, or moving pictures, like film. Cameras are complicated inside, but basically, they catch the light given off by whatever they are pointed at. They use lenses to focus this light, to make an image that can be saved and looked at again.

PHOTO FILM

Film cameras record images on a long strip of plastic. The plastic strip is coated with a chemical that is sensitive to light.

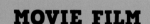

MOVIE FILM

A film camera records a lot of images, one after the other, on very long strips of plastic film. They take 25 separate pictures every second. When the series of images is shown quickly, they all seem to 'join up' and the scene appears to move.

A Frenchman named **Joseph Niépce** took the first photo in 1827. It was not a very reliable process because the light had to enter his camera for 8 hours to make the photo.

GETTING BETTER

After Joseph Niépce's attempts, another Frenchman found a better way to take photographs, in 1839. Louis Daguerre caught his images on silver plates coated with a silver-based chemical that was sensitive to light. It took only a few minutes to make the photo. The same year, a British inventor, William Henry Fox Talbot, took the first ever photograph on paper.

Today's cameras are mostly **digital**. They do not record photos onto plastic film. Instead, they store the images they take digitally. A light-sensitive sensor inside the camera turns the image into a pattern of numbers. The whole photograph is stored as one very long number.

CAMERAS EVERYWHERE

Today, cameras are everywhere. There are cameras in mobile phones and tablets so that people can take hundreds of digital photos and films every day. That does not mean we are any better at photography, though!

IMPORTANT PHOTOGRAPHY

Photography has a lot of uses. As well as recording your holidays and your friends, photos can record important events in the world, and tell other people about them. Wars have been recorded by photographers, who often faced great danger to take their pictures.

Photography has also become a form of art. Many photographers compose their images carefully, which takes great skill.

HEAR THAT?

Our world is almost never silent. By day, we hear the voices of everyone around us, the sounds of cars and planes, machines and music. Even at night, there are animal and bird sounds and the sound of the wind in the trees. Sound is another kind of energy. It is energy that objects produce when they move quickly back and forth, or vibrate.

Sound cannot travel as fast as light, but it is still incredibly fast. It travels faster through warm air than cold air. At 0 °C (32 F), sound travels at 1,190 kph (740 mph).

SOUND WAVES

Sound travels in waves. When the air around an object starts to vibrate, the vibrations spread out through the air like waves in water. They reach our ears and we hear them.

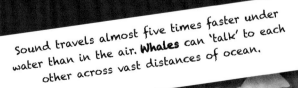

Sound travels almost five times faster under water than in the air. **Whales** can 'talk' to each other across vast distances of ocean.

In **space** there is no air, so there is nothing for sound waves to travel through. This means there is no sound, so space is totally silent.

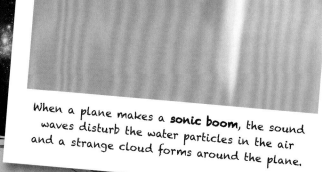

When a plane makes a **sonic boom**, the sound waves disturb the water particles in the air and a strange cloud forms around the plane.

Anything that travels faster than sound is going at a **supersonic speed**. As it reaches the speed of sound, an aircraft makes an incredibly loud bang, called a sonic boom.

MEASURING SOUND

The units used for measuring sound are called decibels (dB). Conversation is about 50 dB. A loud rock concert is about 110 dB. Anything louder than 140 dB can damage your hearing.

A whip makes a snapping sound when you crack it because its tip is moving faster than the speed of sound. It causes a mini sonic boom.

Just as light bounces back off a mirror, sound can bounce back off a hard surface. When this happens, we hear the sound as an **echo**. Try it when you are in a tunnel or cave.

MEASURING WITH SOUND

Echoes can be used to measure distances. Sounds are directed to an object, such as the bottom of the sea. The time they take to come back is recorded. We know the speed of sound, so we can work out how far away the object is. Ships use this method to find underwater objects.

191

SOUND OF MUSIC

Music is a kind of arranged sound. We have learned how to make particular sounds and we put them together in a way that pleases us. We call these sounds 'notes', and we give them names, so everyone knows which sound is which. Maybe you love pop music or classical music or music from countries around the world. Wherever it comes from, it can make you want to dance.

BEAT THE DRUM

A drum has a tight skin that vibrates when it is hit. The air inside the drum vibrates, making the sound.

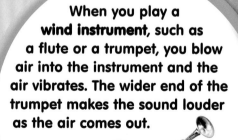

When a **violin** is played, the hairs on the bow are pulled or pushed across the strings on the violin. This makes the strings vibrate, creating sound.

RHYTHM

In music, sounds are arranged into a tune with a regular beat, or rhythm. A catchy rhythm makes everyone want to get up and dance.

When you play a **wind instrument**, such as a flute or a trumpet, you blow air into the instrument and the air vibrates. The wider end of the trumpet makes the sound louder as the air comes out.

Making sounds louder is called **amplification**. Many musical instruments have a part that amplifies their sound. On a guitar, for example, the instrument's large wooden body amplifies the sound made by the strings.

Different **cultures** around the world make their own kinds of music. Some people play wind instruments with their noses, for example, or make music out of hollow trees.

Concert halls are specially designed with curves that spread the sound evenly around the room to every seat. This makes it possible for everyone to hear the music clearly.

PITCH

The highness or lowness of a sound is called its pitch. Musical notes are sounds with a particular pitch. In a stringed instrument, longer strings make sounds with a lower pitch than shorter strings. That is why a double bass makes lower notes than a violin.

09

TECHNICAL TRIUMPHS

Technology is all about how we use science. Scientists develop new technology all the time to make our lives easier, so technology moves forward very quickly. In 10 years' time, the things we think are new and exciting today, will seem old fashioned.

CRAFTY COMPUTERS

Computers are everywhere in today's world. Millions of homes have one and billions of people have a mobile phone with a mini computer inside. Computers control many of the systems that we rely on, such as transport networks, banks and businesses. It is hard to imagine living without them.

A **computer** is an electronic machine that sorts information and does calculations. It obeys instructions that tell it how to present information to us, in a way that we find useful.

HARDWARE OR SOFTWARE

① The hardware of a computer is the actual machine, screen and keyboard. These may be built-in, such as in a laptop and tablet, or separate. The hard disk stores the files of information.

② The software provides the instructions. A computer will run several different kinds of software, to do different jobs, such as playing games or writing stories.

Computers were invented in the 1940s and were so big that each one filled a whole room! Computers today are much smaller and more powerful.

MOVING MOUSE

A mouse moves the pointer around the computer screen, so you can click on where you want to be. At first, the mouse was attached to the computer by a 'tail', but now they are often wireless.

Several computers can be joined together in a **network**. Offices do this so that people can share their information on all the computers. If you have more than one computer in your home, such as a laptop and a tablet, you can link them into a network, too.

The first computer **games**, in the 1980s, were simple. Today, the quality of the graphics and the things you can do in a game are amazing.

BIG SYSTEMS

Computers are powerful enough to cope with big, complicated jobs, such as monitoring all the aircraft coming into and out of an airport. The people in air traffic control must know where every plane is all the time, day and night.

DESIGNED FOR DESIGN

Computers are used in many different industries to design products, from whole buildings to scientific instruments and cars. They can be used to see the designs in 3D and to test how they will work.

ONLINE THE WORLD

The Internet is a huge computer network that covers the whole world. Nobody owns it or controls it. There are rules about how computers connected to it should exchange information, but anyone can share information with the rest of world. The network of websites on the Internet is called the World Wide Web, and many web addresses start with the letters 'www'.

Your computer is not connected directly to the Internet. It is linked by a telephone line to an Internet service provider (ISP). ISPs have very powerful computers, each with an address on the Internet network. The internet pages you look at, go to that address first, then onto you.

GOING WIRELESS

You do not need to be connected to a telephone line by wires to be online. You can connect wirelessly through a radio link. This is how mobile phones and tablet computers access the Internet.

Email, or electronic mail, is a way of sending messages, pictures and sound clips on the Internet, to people anywhere in the world.

There are more than 2.5 billion email users around the world. Together, they send and receive more than 130 billion emails every day.

By 2012, more than 1 billion people had joined the social networking website **Facebook**. If Facebook were a country, it would have the third-largest population in the world.

Facebook was started in the United States in 2004 by Mark Zuckerberg and his college roommates. They wanted a way to connect with their friends online. Today Facebook is one of the biggest companies in the world and Mark Zuckerberg is a billionaire.

TWITTER

Twitter started in 2006. It is a network for sending short messages, called Tweets. Tweets must be no more than 140 characters long. Today, there are more than 200 million Twitter users worldwide and more than 500 million Tweets are sent every day.

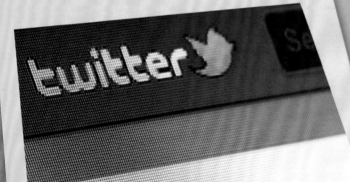

We produce so much **data** that it can be hard to find space on your computer to store it all. Many people store their stuff in a 'cloud'.

More and more people are doing their **shopping online**. You order foods from a supermarket's website, for example, and it delivers shopping to your home. It saves you time and it causes less pollution from car journeys.

TELEPHONES

Telephones were first invented in 1876, but the scientist who invented them, Alexander Graham Bell, would not be familiar with the phones we all use today. Telephone messages can be carried in two ways, along cables or by radio signals. Mobile phones use radio signals. The main telephone in your home may use cables. Telephones can connect people on opposite sides of the world, in an instant. They keep us all in touch with each other.

When you press the number keys on a phone with a cable, you are sending a **signal** along the line to a local 'exchange'. From there, it travels on to other exchanges until it reaches the phone you are calling. The cables are made of thin glass strands that send the signals at super-high speed.

LONG DISTANCE

If you are calling someone very far away, your message may be bounced off a satellite in space and back to Earth near the person you are calling. It takes only a second or two.

LIFE ONLINE

Phones that can use the Internet are called smartphones. They do not just make calls. They can be used for sending emails, browsing the Internet, taking photos and videos, using apps and playing music and games.

Mobiles and other wireless phones send phone messages as **radio signals** through the air. They are picked up by transmitters, which pass them on to the phone you are calling.

An **app** is computer software that is designed to run on a mobile phone or tablet. App is short for 'application'. There are apps for many things, such as gaming, reading newspapers and shopping. In 2013, more than 100 billion apps were downloaded worldwide.

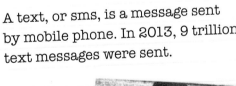

The mobile phones we use today contain **computers** that are more powerful than those used for the *Apollo 11* moon landings in 1969.

HUNGRY FOR APPLE

In 2012, Apple sold 340,000 iPhones a day. By March 2015, Apple had sold more than 700 million iPhones.

TEXTING FRENZY

A text, or sms, is a message sent by mobile phone. In 2013, 9 trillion text messages were sent.

Many businesses now want us to use our phones to buy things. They put a special **barcode** in their adverts. If you scan it with your phone, you are connected to a website where you can find out more about the product, or buy it.

TELEVISION AND RADIO

The first radio signals were sent just over 100 years ago. At first, they could be sent only over short distances. Today, we can broadcast radio and television shows from one side of the world to the other. There are many radio and TV channels to choose from, so anyone can find something they like.

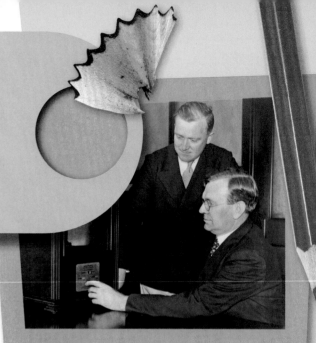

FIRST TELEVISION

The first television was made by John Logie Baird in 1924. He used some very odd things to make it, such as cardboard, a tin, knitting needles and wax. The one above was made in 1931. The first US television station began in 1928. The BBC broadcast its first television show in 1930.

SENDING SIGNALS

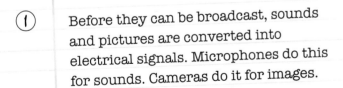

① Before they can be broadcast, sounds and pictures are converted into electrical signals. Microphones do this for sounds. Cameras do it for images.

② The electrical signals are then sent by radio waves. They are picked up by receivers across the land and sent on to our homes. Some radio and TV broadcasts are sent by satellite dishes on Earth to satellites in space and back down to Earth again.

Until the 1970s, all TV shows were in **black and white**. Technology had not worked out how to send pictures in other colours. It was not much good for nature shows.

Remote controls were invented in the 1980s. Before then, you changed channels and adjusted the volume using knobs on the front or side of your television.

Most television **broadcasting** is now done digitally. The sounds and pictures are sent as a 'code' of millions of digits, either 0 or 1. This code is carried by radio waves.

SATELLITE TV

Satellite television bounces the sound and picture signals off satellites up in space. The signals are received directly into your home by a small dish, fixed to the outside wall or roof of the building.

The most-watched TV shows are usually global **sports** events such as the Olympic Games or the FIFA World Cup.

Many people use the television for playing **games**, for example on an Xbox or PlayStation. The high quality of the screen and the sound make it even more exciting.

FLYING HIGH

People have always dreamed of flying and seeing the world from up in the sky. That became possible just over 100 years ago. Since then, we have invented more and more powerful planes and other flying machines, too. Some of them have military uses or are used to transport goods. Others carry people around the world for holidays and business.

The first **aircrafts** were built by the Wright brothers. They had propellers and were made of wood, wire and string. They made the first-ever powered and controlled flight in 1903.

LIFT OFF!

The first aircraft ever to fly was a hot air balloon. It was built by the two Montgolfier brothers in 1783. It carried a sheep, a chicken and a duck. The flight lasted 8 minutes. Later that year, two men went up in it. They were the first people to fly.

Planes have fixed wings and an engine. The engine moves the plane forward, so the wings can create lift and overcome the force of gravity, to lift off the ground.

FLYING SOLO

Amelia Earhart was the first woman to fly alone across the Atlantic Ocean, in 1932. It took her around 15 hours. Later, she attempted to fly around the world alone, but her plane disappeared over the Pacific Ocean and was never found.

Concorde was a passenger aircraft that flew faster than sound. It could fly from London to New York in about 3 hours. A normal plane takes 7 or 8 hours to do this journey.

Helicopters get off the ground using huge overhead propellers. They can move easily back and forth, and from side to side. They can also hover, which planes cannot do.

RECORD BREAKER

The fastest speed ever reached by an aircraft was by a Lockheed SR-71 Blackbird. This military jet flew at 3,530 kph (2,193 mph). It was used as a spy plane.

The world's biggest **passenger aircraft** is the Airbus A380. It has four engines, two decks and a wide body. It can carry up to 853 people.

NO PILOT

Drones are aircraft that have no pilot. They are flown by computers operated by people on the ground. They are used by the military to look at, or bomb, areas that are under enemy control.

SUPER STRUCTURES

Throughout history, people have been making more and more impressive structures. As cities have grown, we have made churches, bridges and towers reaching higher and higher up into the sky. Today, our knowledge of engineering allows us to build massive skyscrapers that are hundreds of floors tall.

The **Eiffel Tower** in Paris, France, held the record for the world's tallest building from 1889 until 1930. It is 324 m (1,063 ft) tall.

FIT FOR A KING

The ancient **Egyptians** built huge pyramids as tombs for their kings, or pharaohs. The Great Pyramid at Giza was completed in about 2560 BCE (more than 4,500 years ago). It was 146 m (479 ft) high and the world's tallest building for more than 3,800 years altogether!

The **Empire State Building** in New York City was completed in 1931. It was the first building to have more than 100 floors. It is 381 m (1,250 ft) high. It has a viewing platform, which gives fantastic views of the other skyscrapers in New York.

The medieval cathedrals of Europe towered above other buildings in their towns. They were built by master architects and craftsmen. The spire of **Rouen Cathedral** in France is 151 m (495 ft) tall.

A LONG WAY DOWN

The Grand Canyon is an amazing rock valley in Arizona, United States. This natural wonder is 446 km (277 miles) long and more than 1.6 km (1 mile) deep in places. A U-shaped bridge has been built that hangs out over the edge. The Grand Canyon Skywalk has a glass floor, so you can see 1.2 km (4,000 ft) down to the ground.

In a **suspension bridge**, the road part hangs below long cables attached to vertical towers. The world's third-longest suspension bridge is Denmark's Great Belt Bridge.

TALLEST STRUCTURE

The tallest human-made structure in the world is Burj Khalifa in Dubai, United Arab Emirates. It stands 829.8 m (2,722 ft) high, and it was opened in 2010. It also has 163 floors, which is the most floors of any building. Its observation deck is on the 148th floor.

EDEN PROJECT

Some structures are remarkable not because they are the biggest or tallest, but because they are so clever. The Eden Project in Cornwall, England, was built in an old mine pit. It contains plants from all over the world for visitors to see. Its giant greenhouses, or biomes, are made of hundreds of large hexagonal plastic shapes joined by a steel frame.

MACHINES IN ACTION

Machines make work easier, whether it is a pair of scissors or a massive crane. We put a small force into a machine, and get a much bigger force out of it. Large construction projects need big machines. We have invented some really enormous machines to help us build skyscrapers, tunnels and bridges. We have also invented some very tiny machines, for example, to help us in medicine.

Gears are used in machines to change speed. They do this by changing the size of the turning force inside the machine. They are used in cars and clocks.

Cranes are superstrong lifting machines. They are used in construction to lift pieces of new buildings into position. They are also used for loading goods onto ships at the docks.

MINING FOR COAL

Coal mines take coal out of the earth from deep underground. These massive drills are used to bore into the rock, to break up the coal so it can be collected and brought to the surface.

A MASSIVE BANG

The largest machine ever built is the Large Hadron Collider, in Geneva, Switzerland. It is made of a circular, underground tunnel 27 km (16.7 miles) long. It was built to conduct a science experiment that makes particles collide almost at the speed of light.

These huge oil **pumps** are bringing up oil from deep underground. They work night and day.

DRIVERLESS TRAINS

The Dubai Metro system is the longest automated rail network in the world. Its 87 trains run without drivers on tracks that cover 75 km (47 miles).

Wheels are simple machines. They are used to move heavy weights a long distance. Join two wheels with a rod, called an axle, add a box on top and you have a cart.

Did you know?

Scientists have invented a tiny machine to unblock blood vessels. It uses a small balloon to open up the blood vessel from the inside, then props it open with a tube, called a stent.

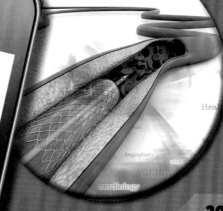

COOL CARS

Cars have transformed the way we live. Around 120 years ago, they had just been invented and hardly anybody had one. Today, there are more than 1 billion cars on our roads. They come in all shapes and sizes and have four wheels powered by an engine that usually runs on petrol, gasoline or diesel. Some modern cars are powered by electricity instead and this technology is developing fast.

BLACK OR BLACK

The Model T Ford was one of the first cars to be made on a production line, in 1908. This made it affordable so more people bought them. Its maker Henry Ford said, 'You can have it in any colour as long as it's black!'

CALL FOR THE CAR!

Driverless cars work by sensors that take thousands of pictures of the road ahead to decide how to travel safely. Google is working on an electric model that has no steering wheel or pedals.

Some of the cars built for land-speed **racing** look more like rockets as they zoom along. They are called turbojets.

POLLUTION PROBLEMS

When car engines burn fuel, they cause pollution in the air. This is bad for people's health and builds up in the atmosphere. We need to make fewer journeys and have cleaner cars to solve this problem.

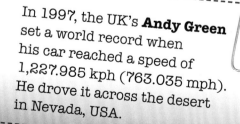

In 1997, the UK's **Andy Green** set a world record when his car reached a speed of 1,227.985 kph (763.035 mph). He drove it across the desert in Nevada, USA.

Formula One cars feature some amazing science and technology, which helps them to stay on the track while they move at incredible speeds.

GENIUS DRIVER

In the 2004 Formula One season, Germany's Michael Schumacher won an incredible 13 races out of 18.

CAR STATS

① The average car has 30,000 parts. It is no wonder that cars break down sometimes!

② The world's fastest production car is the Bugatti Veyron Super Sport. It has a top speed of 431 kph (268 mph).

About 165,000 **new cars** are made in the world every day.

SHIPS AND BOATS

About three-quarters of Earth's surface is covered with seas, so we have invented brilliant ways to cross them in boats and ships. Ships can carry loads much bigger than lorries, trains or planes. The biggest ones can make longer journeys, too. Boats and ships are useful for massive jobs, but they can also be great fun.

Galleons were large ships that sailed the seas in the 1500s to 1700s. The *Mayflower*, which took the first pilgrims from England to settle in America in 1620, was a galleon.

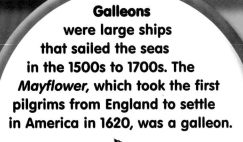

ANCIENT WARSHIPS

The ancient Greeks had impressive fighting ships, called triremes. These long sailing ships had three rows of oars. A spike at the front could ram into enemy ships.

AIRCRAFT CARRIERS

Aircraft carriers are massive warships. They carry military aircraft to where they need to be, as well as many crew. Their decks act like a runway for the jets to take off and land. They are more than 12 tennis courts long.

Oil tankers are some of the biggest machines ever made. Some of them are so huge they could fit five football pitches on deck. They transport oil around the world.

Some high-speed **motorboats** are built for having fun. They power through the waves at top speeds. Sometimes, they compete in competitions. They can also be used for rescue operations when other boats are in trouble.

At the Poles, ships need to be able to cross the sea without becoming stuck in the ice. Huge **icebreaker ships** are reinforced, so they can carve a channel through the ice as they go. They ram the ice, shattering it into pieces.

TECHNICAL TRIUMPHS

Kayaks are rowing boats that use single paddles instead of oars. They can go incredibly fast through the water, especially through white water in a sporting competition.

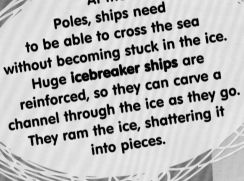

Passenger ships carry tourists on cruises. The Oasis of the Seas can take 6,360 passengers and 2,394 crew. The liner even has an outdoor park on board!

BOATS WITH WINGS?

A hydrofoil is a boat that flies in water. It has wing-like foils on the bottom and as it picks up speed, the foils lift the boat out of the water. Hydrofoils are mostly used as ferries.

REAL ROBOTS

Robots make fantastic toys, but they are brilliant for so many other things, too. They can do things that are too dangerous for us, or that need great strength. Building a robot needs a mix of electrical engineering and computer science, making it one of the most cutting-edge areas of technology today.

AI

Will robots ever be as clever as humans? The science of this is called artificial intelligence (AI). Experts are working on ways to make a computer that can think for itself, just like our brains. They have not cracked it yet.

A massive industrial **robotic arm** was built in the United States in 2008. It could lift the equivalent of an average-size caravan in one go.

In 2014, a robot called *Cubestormer 3* solved the difficult puzzle of a Rubik's Cube in 3.253 seconds. The fastest time to solve the puzzle by a human is 5.55 seconds.

BOT FACTS

① Robots are great for doing the jobs we do not like, such as cleaning the floor. There are even robot vacuum cleaners that work by remote control while you relax.

② Robots are used for jobs that are dangerous for humans. The Dragon Runner robot can be thrown into buildings or caves to clear mines and other explosives. It is incredibly tough and can even operate upside down.

③ Most car factories use robots in their automated production lines. The robots can carry parts and put them together without ever getting tired.

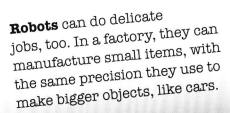

Robots can do delicate jobs, too. In a factory, they can manufacture small items, with the same precision they use to make bigger objects, like cars.

STAR WARS

Two of the most famous robots in cinema history are R2-D2 and C-3PO from *Star Wars*. They were brave and clever, and played a big role in saving the galaxy time and time again.

Robot **cameras** can fly over places that humans cannot reach. They can also take pictures to give us information. This can be really useful after a natural disaster, such as a flood, for example.

Nao is a **humanoid** robot that is built to be your friend. It also competes in the RoboCup soccer championship.

The inventor and artist **Leonardo da Vinci**, drew up plans for a reinforced humanoid machine in 1495. He made drawings of the human body to understand how it worked from the inside.

COOL INVENTIONS

Ever since humans first evolved, we have been inventing things. First, we learned how to sharpen stones to make tools and weapons and how to hunt for our food. Then, we invented places to live and ways to grow food to feed more people. New inventions are constantly making our lives safer, richer and more fun.

In 1895, Wilhelm Roentgen discovered X-rays. He took the first ever X-ray photos, which were of his wife's hand. X-rays made it possible to see inside the body without cutting it open.

SAVING LIVES

In 1796, scientist Edward Jenner invented the first ever vaccine, for a disease called smallpox. He saw that giving someone a small dose of a disease protected his or her body from getting the full, harmful version. Now, millions of people worldwide are given vaccines to protect them from dangerous diseases.

LOOK ME UP!

In 1878, the first telephone book was invented. As the telephone was so new and hardly anybody had one, it contained only 50 names.

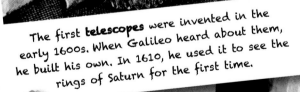

The first **telescopes** were invented in the early 1600s. When Galileo heard about them, he built his own. In 1610, he used it to see the rings of Saturn for the first time.

The first **toothbrush** was invented in 1498 in China. Before then, people kept their teeth clean by chewing on a stick until it became frayed like a brush. The first brushes used hairs from the neck of a pig.

Tim Berners-Lee invented the World Wide Web. The Internet already existed, but he came up with the idea of hypertext (text on a screen with links to other text in other websites).

MEDICAL TREATMENT

Marie Curie was a scientist who discovered radioactivity and used it to destroy cancer cells growing in the body. She was the first woman to win the Nobel Prize, and she won it twice.

PRINTING

Two of the most revolutionary inventions were the printing press and moveable type. A printing press is used to make copies of a page. Until it was invented, books were handwritten. In the 1400s, Johannes Gutenberg invented typesetting, where individual letters are put together to form words and blocks of text. They are covered in ink and pressed onto paper.

Trainers were invented in the 1970s. Today, so many young people never wear leather shoes that the Army says their feet are too soft for traditional military boots.

TELLING THE TIME

We use time to order what happens into the past, the present and the future. Time is also useful for measuring the speed at which things move. The first ways we measured time were ingenious, but not very accurate. Today, we can measure time incredibly accurately.

The world is split into 24 **time zones**, so that the sun is directly overhead at 12 noon wherever you are. Places in the East have their noon before places further West.

SUN TIME

The first clocks used the way the sun passes across the sky to tell the time. The shadow cast by the metal arm on a sundial, moves round through the day.

In a **sand clock**, fine sand flows from one glass bulb into another through a narrow tube. It is called an hourglass.

Southern Ocean

People have arranged days into blocks of seven, called **weeks**, for thousands of years. The Romans named the days of the week after the sun, the moon and the planets.

The **second** is the unit of time that also sets all the others. It is set according to 200 atomic clocks in 50 different laboratories around the world.

Clocks were first created by monks living in Italy in the 1300s. They wanted to measure the lengths of time between each session of prayers in chapel. They invented a machine that rang a bell every hour. Before long, clocks were put up in public places all over Europe.

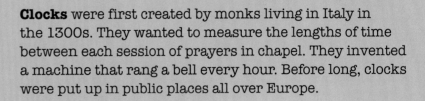

ATOMIC CLOCK

An atomic clock is not mechanical, but works with atoms instead. It counts how many times an atom vibrates back and forth. It is the most accurate kind of clock there is.

Planck time is the smallest known unit of time. It measures the amount of time it takes light to travel one Planck length. This is a distance so small that it cannot be measured.

 **Smart watches** do not just tell you the time. You can use them to go online, measure your heart rate and many other things.

FANTASTIC FUTURE

Scientists of all kinds are busy working on inventions and developments that will change our world in the future. By the time you are an adult, some of them will have become a normal part of everyday life. Others will take longer. However, it is certain that our brilliant, inventive minds will carry on looking for ways to make our lives better.

In 2010, US President **Barack Obama** set a goal of launching a manned mission to Mars in the 2030s. There are some plans by a private company to do just that in the 2020s. If you decide to go, it will be a one-way ticket, because it is too far and too expensive to come back.

SPACE PLANES

Space planes are reusable rockets. They would make it much cheaper to go into space, so missions could take off more often. If we are going to live on Mars, we will need them.

THAT'S FAST!

One US inventor is working on a new transport system called Hyperloop. It involves train-like vehicles going through tubes with no friction. That would allow them to reach speeds of up to 966 kph (600 mph).

3D printing prints out solid, 3D objects. This will make it possible to print replacement parts for machines, and even for humans.

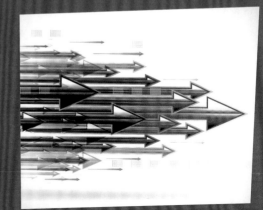

Graphene is a new human-made material, invented in 2004. It is only one atom thick, but it is stronger than steel and can be made into huge sheets.

Nanorobots are mini machines that are small enough to enter the body. These robots will be used to repair damage or to deliver drugs.

GROWING MEAT?

Scientists have been experimenting with new techniques for 'growing' meat. They have used special cells, called stem cells, from animals to grow new muscle tissue.

This lab-grown meat could become more efficient to produce than the traditional way, which uses a lot of land, water and resources.

BETTER CROPS

Scientists now understand the genetic code of wheat, so they are developing new, improved varieties that will produce more grains per plant. They are also working on a chemical that can be sprayed onto crops to make them more resistant to drought.

Vehicles powered by **hydrogen fuel** could become popular in the future. These vehicles will be pollution-free as their only waste product is water.

INDEX

Picture Credits